**Wooden Spoon**
The children's charity of rugby

# RUGBYWORLD
# Yearbook 2014

### Editor
## Ian Robertson

### Photographs
### Getty Images

Published in the UK in 2013 by
Lennard Publishing, an imprint of
Lennard Associates Ltd,
Mackerye End,
Harpenden, Herts AL5 5DR
email: orders@lennardqap.co.uk

Distributed by G2 Entertainment
c/o Orca Book Services
160 Eastern Avenue, Milton Park
Abingdon, OX14 4SB

ISBN: 978-1-85291-156-0

Production editor: Chris Marshall
Text and cover design: Paul Cooper

Caricature of Adam Jones on page 19 by John Ireland

The publishers would like to thank Getty Images for providing most of the photographs for
this book.  The publishers would also like to thank Carl Sutton of Howzat Travel, Neil
Kennedy, Rugby Matters, Fotosport UK, Fotosport Italy, Inpho Photography, Chris Thau and
Wooden Spoon for additional material.

Printed and bound in the UK
by Butler, Tanner and Dennis

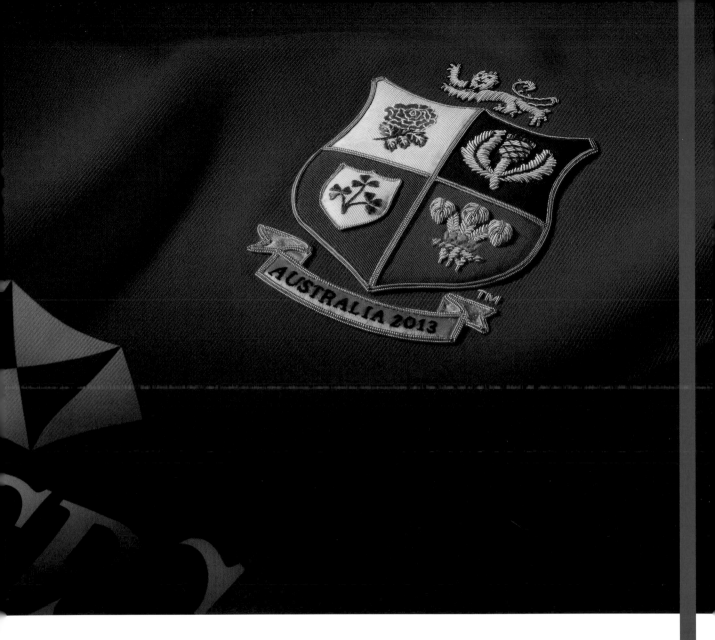

# THE LEGEND LIVES ON...

HSBC are **proud** to have supported THE BRITISH & IRISH LIONS on yet another *legendary* journey down under.

*Congratulations* to all the players and staff who made it happen.

youtube.com/LionsHSBC

**PRINCIPAL PARTNER**

*Fig. 1:* Typical British and Irish Profits
(hoping for some tries)

Discipline, intense concentration and effort – sound familiar? All these elements are just as important on the Profit hunting ground as they are on the rugby pitch.

If you'd like to find out more about Hunting Profits please contact your financial adviser, call 0800 092 2051 or visit artemis.co.uk.

ARTEMIS
The PROFIT Hunter

The value of an investment, and any income from it, can fall as well as rise as a result of market and currency fluctuations and you may not get back the amount originally invested. Please remember that past performance is not a guide to the future.

Issued by Artemis Fund Managers Ltd which is authorised and regulated by the Financial Conduct Authority (www.fca.org.uk), 25 The North Colonnade, Canary Wharf, London E14 5HS.

# Contents

# FOREWORD

## by HRH THE PRINCESS ROYAL

**BUCKINGHAM PALACE**

HRH The Princess Royal,
Royal Patron of Wooden Spoon.

Since its origins back in 1983 Wooden Spoon has enhanced the lives of over one million disadvantaged children and young people throughout the British Isles. Now in its 30th year, Wooden Spoon has donated over £20 million to schools, hospitals, respite homes and hospices, other children's charities and community projects such as Game On! The money Wooden Spoon has raised helps children and young people who face a multitude of different physical, mental and social difficulties.

Despite the challenging economy, over the last year Wooden Spoon has committed over £1.3 million and opened more than sixty projects. This is the largest number of projects delivered in a single year in the history of the charity, which is most encouraging as the benevolent work of charities such as Wooden Spoon is needed more than ever. As Wooden Spoon enters its 30th year we can reflect with pride on the achievements of Wooden Spoon thanks to the selfless support of its volunteers, members and supporters who all give their time freely for the benefit of others.

As Patron of Wooden Spoon I wish everyone involved with fundraising through this celebratory year great success and a lot of fun and I would like to thank you for your interest and enthusiasm. This is a unique and vibrant charity that has achieved much, but can and will achieve a lot more with your support both now and in the future.

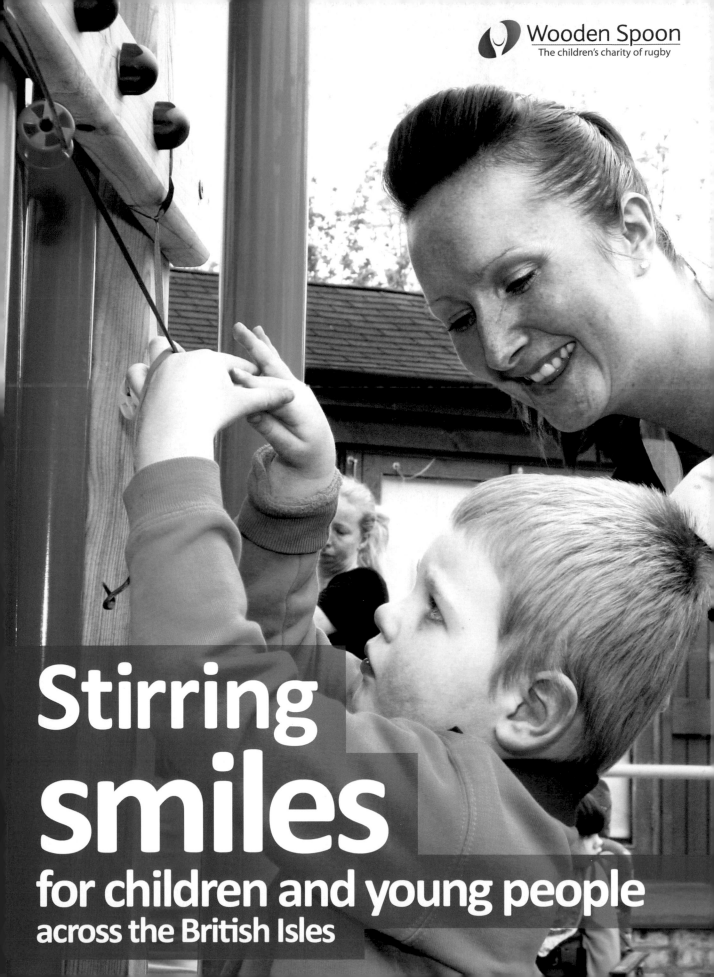

**Wooden Spoon**
The children's charity of rugby

# Stirring smiles
## for children and young people
### across the British Isles

# Wooden Spoon
The children's charity of rugby

# Who we are

**In the UK, one child in every hundred suffers from a lifelong disability that will profoundly affect his or her ability to lead a full and happy life.**

**More than 3.5 million children grow up in low income households or live in an environment where they are subjected to poverty of aspiration.**

**Over 1 million young people aged between 16-19 are not in full time employment, education or training.**

At Wooden Spoon, we believe that all children and young people deserve the chance to live happy fulfilled lives regardless of the challenges they may face. Wooden Spoon harnesses the spirit and values of rugby to give disadvantaged children and young people a chance to achieve their full potential in life.

Wooden Spoon is a children's charity founded in 1983 that is dedicated to helping disadvantaged children and young people across the British Isles live happier, richer lives. We partner with the UK rugby community, receiving invaluable support for our activities and the opportunity to raise awareness of the work we do. In doing so, we involve some of rugby's top sporting role models in making a difference in the lives of young people in need.

We proudly comprise over 40 regional volunteer committees, a central national team and over 10,000 members. All regional committees undertake many local fundraising activities and only spend the money raised on projects in their local community.

During our first 30 years, over a million young people benefitted from more than £20 million of charitable support thanks to the efforts of our staff, volunteers and supporters. We are proud of our legacy, the work we do, and our ambitious plans for the future.

## Winners
of the Spirit of Rugby
Award 2011

In October 2011 Wooden Spoon were awarded the Spirit of Rugby award. This prestigious award recognises the incredible feats that can be achieve through rugby both on and off the field, and recognises the incredible fundraising of Wooden Spoon and its volunteers for more that 30 years of work with disadvantaged children and young people throughout the British Isles.

# What we do

We organise our own fundraising initiatives, raise the money and spend it where it is most needed. Over the years, our donations have diversified from capital projects such as medical treatment and recovery centres, sports and activity areas, sensory rooms and gardens, playgrounds and hydrotherapy pools to include outreach programmes for young people in their communities.

## Wooden Spoon has funded hundreds of projects across the British Isles such as:

**The Hitz** programme works to initiate behaviour change and foster confidence in disenfranchised young people aged 11 to 19 from challenging backgrounds; encouraging them to remain in or re-enter education, undertake apprenticeships or vocational training and enter paid employment. The Hitz programme is Premiership Rugby's flagship and award-winning social-inclusion programme delivered by Aviva Premiership Rugby clubs, with learning provision provided by YMCA training and funded by national partners Comic Relief and Wooden Spoon.

**Guernsey Extreme Association** received £50,000 towards the build of the Jubilee Skate Park. The Jubilee Skate Park is situated within the grounds of a municipal sports complex and is designed to accommodate skateboarders of all levels of expertise and the runs are specifically designed to be disabled-accessed, including wheelchair ramping.

**Hereward College in Warwickshire** benefitted from a donation of £12,000 towards the build of the 'Wooden Spoon Suite'. Hareward College is a general further education college for 250 day students, and 50 residential students, all aged 16-19 years who suffer from a range of serious mental and physical disabilities including Cerebral Palsy, Muscular Dystrophy, Asperger's Syndrome and Autism.

**Creative Youth Network in Bristol City Centre** received £28,500 towards the build of disabled-friendly washrooms along with the purchase of the main doors which were specially designed to be electronically controlled, with wheelchair ramps and low-level, push-button activation panels.

**PACT based in Reading** benefitted from £10,000 for the creation of a specially designed therapy counselling room. Unlike Social Services input to the adoption process which tends to be short term, PACT recognises the traumas and relationship problems that adoption generally causes throughout the child's early and teenage years. Apart from the careful matching of children to parents, PACT provides counselling and therapeutic sessions for both children and parents.

**Ferring Country Centre in Sussex** received £14,000 towards the build of the Wooden Spoon Pavilion. The pavilion will act as a focus for the centre's small animal farm and provide an educational facility for people with learning difficulties and visiting school children.

Wooden Spoon
The children's charity of rugby

# What events do we run

### Wooden Spoon fundraisers
Wooden Spoon volunteer committees organise hundreds of fundraising events every year including golf days, rugby matches, physical challenges, summer fetes, balls, dinners and many others that raise the crucial funds for the charity and appeal to potential supporters.

### Wooden Spoon bespoke charity challenges
We run a series of bespoke physical challenges across the UK and overseas that include.

### The Ford Ranger Great Lakeland Challenge
The longest, highest and steepest challenge. Participants canoe England's longest lake, cycle England's steepest passes and conquer England's highest peak all in just 12 hours.

### Four Peaks Challenge
Our most successful and well-known challenge. Participants climb four of the highest mountains in Scotland, England, Wales and Ireland, a total of 14,000 feet and drive the 1,900 miles between them all within 48 hours.

### London 2 Monte Carlo Cycle Challenge
One of our most taxing challenges. Participants hit the road from the centre of London and cycle 760 miles in 8.5 days through some of the most stunning scenery until finally arriving in Grand Casino Square.

### London Marathon
Run 26.2 miles for Wooden Spoon in the world's biggest marathon. Wooden Spoon has 15 coveted Gold Bond Places for the London Marathon.

# The story behind Wooden Spoon

A wonderful legacy emerged in 1983 after England's rugby team was defeated by the Irish. Drowning their sorrows in a Dublin bar, a group of fans was presented with a wooden spoon by the victorious Irish to symbolise a winless Five Nations Championship.

Accepting the spoon with good humour and grace, the fans then resolved to hold a charity golf match to see who would have the honour of keeping the spoon. The match raised in excess of £8,000 and the money was donated to provide the children of Park School, Aylesbury, with a Sunshine Bus. This was to be the of first many Wooden Spoon charitable projects.

# Our Royal Patron

Our Royal Patron is HRH The Princess Royal who gives generously of her time.

## Our Rugby Patrons

The RFU, WRU, SRU, IRFU, RFL all support us in our charitable work.

# COMMENT
# & FEATURES

# Lions Triumphant the 2013 Tour to Australia

## by IAN ROBERTSON

'Alex Corbisiero had scored a try almost from the kick-off. The referee Romain Poite kept penalising the broken and humiliated Wallaby scrum'

The 2013 tour of Australia was a major and significant milestone in the history of the British & Irish Lions. To put it into perspective this was only the fifth time in 23 major Lions tours during the last 105 years that the Lions have won a Test series. It is the first time the Lions have won a series in the 21st century and it is also the first series victory since 1997, when they beat South Africa by two Tests to one.

The magnitude of the achievement should not be underestimated, because every recent Lions campaign in the professional era has become increasingly tough. In 1974 Willie John McBride led the Lions on the greatest tour of all time. They played a total of 22 matches, winning 21 and drawing the final Test after triumphing in the first three Tests. The 'Invincibles' of 1974 were on tour for over three months. Since 1983 the number of matches has been drastically reduced, making it almost but not quite impossible for the Lions to win a series.

The 2013 tour to Australia was cut back to just nine matches, which is the smallest number ever. The Lions played only five games in Australia before the first Test. It is not easy to give all 37 players enough game time before selecting the best possible Test team. There was also a warm-up match against the Barbarians in Hong Kong which hardly stretched the Lions, who romped to an easy win by 59 points to 8, including eight tries.

In the first game in Australia against a very weak Western Force team in Perth, the margin of victory was even bigger – 69 points to 17. The Queensland Reds then gave the Lions a genuine challenge before losing by 22 points to 12. There followed a 64-0 massacre of the Combined Country XV in Newcastle and a hammering of the New South Wales Waratahs in Sydney by 47 points to 17. With the Test team rested for the match against the Brumbies in Canberra the Lions lost 14-12, but this game and the result bore no relevance to the first Test four days later.

The first Test squad looked strong and the Wallabies turned up in Brisbane seriously short of match practice. They had not played a Test for over six months, but they trailed only 13-12 at half-time after two great tries from their new wing Israel Folau. George North scored a brilliant try for the Lions midway through the first half, and early in the second half Alex Cuthbert scored another. Leigh Halfpenny converted both and also kicked three penalties.

The Lions deserved their 23-21 win, but they were fortunate that Kurtley Beale missed a late penalty kick in front of the posts from 45 metres when he slipped and lost his footing in the act of striking the ball. The Lions had the better of the forward battle, looking solid in the scrums and on top at the line out. The backs created two wonderful tries and there was every hope they would build on this performance to wrap up the series in Melbourne.

On the downside Paul O'Connell fractured his right arm and was ruled out of the rest of the tour. There was one other important footnote. The Australian captain, James Horwill, was cited after the game for allegedly stamping on Alun Wyn Jones at a ruck. It looked very bad on the television replays, but surprisingly he was cleared to play in the second Test.

**ABOVE** George North leaves Berrick Barnes flailing on his way to scoring his memorable solo try in the first Test.

**FACING PAGE** Tour skipper Sam Warburton and his pride after victory in the third Test.

After an easy 35-0 win against the Rebels in midweek, the Lions made several changes for the second Test. In the backs Alex Cuthbert and Mike Phillips were replaced by Tommy Bowe and Ben Youngs. In the pack Alex Corbisiero and Paul O'Connell were out injured and Mako Vunipola and Geoff Parling came into the team. At blind-side flanker, Dan Lydiate was preferred to Tom Croft. The Wallabies kept the same pack and replaced their two injured backs from the first Test – Kurtley Beale started in place of Berrick Barnes and Joe Tomane took over from Digby Ioane.

The Lions were favourites, but they struggled in the scrums and lacked the creative energy in the backs which they had shown in the first Test. They led 12-9 at half-time, Leigh Halfpenny kicking four penalties for the Lions, and Christian Leali'ifano getting three for Australia. Halfpenny added another penalty midway through the second half for a 15-9 lead, but lacking possession the Lions were trapped in their own half for the final 20 minutes. It was a game of frantic, desperate intensity, but the Wallabies wrapped it up a few minutes from the end with Leali'ifano converting a try by Adam Ashley-Cooper for a one-point, 16-15, victory. Just as Beale missed a kick in the last minute of the first Test, so did Leigh Halfpenny in the second Test. His kick from near the halfway line fell short. The first two Test matches were tantalisingly close and could so easily have each produced different winners.

The third Test was not close! The Lions produced a magnificent display of scintillating rugby to overwhelm the Wallabies in the most comprehensive manner imaginable. Since the first tour in 1888, the highest Lions score in a Test was 31 points against Australia in 1966. In Sydney in 2013 they set a new record of 41 points, including four great tries. It was a remarkable effort by the Lions side – all the more so because of the highly controversial axing of Brian O'Driscoll not just from the team but from the Test squad.

The rugby world was shocked by this decision. Hoards of great names leapt to support O'Driscoll, including the All Black legend Dan Carter plus two former Lions coaches, Sir Ian McGeechan and Sir Clive Woodward, who all felt he should have definitely been in the squad. O'Driscoll was dropped for the first and only time in his long and distinguished 14-year career.

Every other decision in changing the team for the third Test was good and Warren Gatland would take huge pride he got it right. He beefed up and improved the pack by bringing in Alex Corbisiero and Richard Hibbard in the front row and Sean O'Brien and Toby Faletau in the back row. Alun Wyn Jones took over the captaincy from Sam Warburton, who had had a tremendous match in the second Test before damaging his hamstring. The new captain was to enjoy probably the most memorable day of his rugby career.

The Lions forwards totally dominated the scrum and the breakdown. The 35,000 Lions supporters all draped in red witnessed one of the best and most convincing Lions performances in history. From their outstanding forward platform they led 19-3 approaching half-time. Alex Corbisiero had scored a try almost from the kick-off; Leigh Halfpenny had kicked the conversion and four penalties. The referee Romain Poite kept penalising the broken and humiliated Wallaby scrum.

The Wallabies staged a comeback with a try, a conversion and two penalties in the space of seven minutes, but this recovery was short-lived. The Lions took total control and scored three great tries in 12 minutes through Jonny Sexton, George North and Jamie Roberts. With two of these converted and another penalty added, Leigh Halfpenny – the Man of the Match and the Player of the Series – scored 21 points in the 41-16 victory. It was a fantastic day for the Lions, to end what had been a roller-coaster ride over the previous three weeks.

**BELOW** Loose-head Alex Corbisiero touches down for the Lions just moments into the third Test in Sydney.

**FACING PAGE** Adam Jones started all three Tests at tight-head and was the cornerstone of the Lions scrum.

When the Lions set off to New Zealand in four years' time, they will not only have topped 40 points for the first time in a Test match but they will land in Auckland having won three of their last four Test matches – the last Test in South Africa in 2009 and two of the three in Australia in 2013.

Almost shades of the 1974 Lions! Well done to Warren Gatland and his coaching team plus Dr James Robson and his medical team – and above all the players.

They were a very special Pride of Lions.

# The Best 2½ Weeks of My Life
## a Lions Diary   by DAVID STEWART

'In Sydney the wide smiles spread across thousands of faces atop red shirts told their own stories: "We are so pleased to have been here to see that"'

This article has had three introductory lines. The first, inspired by sights at Heathrow and on the journey to Brisbane, was 'Lions supporters are easy to spot'. The second was going to be 'The Welsh are amazing'. But looking back at the tour, only one form of words provides an accurate summary: 'This was the best 2½ weeks of my life'.

It started on a warm Wednesday evening at Heathrow. Lions supporters are easy to spot. They tend to be of a certain age, gender and dress sense. Outer garments range between a tour-group polo shirt freshly out of the wrapper, a colourful club blazer, and basic drinking gear; 'Man at Oxfam' makes an occasional appearance. By Abu Dhabi, many of the thirsty ones were well refreshed. By Singapore, a few were hanging on by their fingertips. As the last leg to Brisbane started, it was amusing to eavesdrop upon a younger member of the species 'charm' the hostess into a couple more: 'Where are you from? Oh, Middlesbrough ... I was there once ... any chance of another Foster's?'

Here, it may be prudent to make the point the great Gareth Edwards does at the end of his autobiography, after a number of chapters had described various bacchanalian activities. Rugby touring involves alcohol; sometimes quite a lot of it.

An early reading of *The Courier-Mail* was a shock. Rugby league enjoyed nine pages, racing got seven, and union less than one. In Queensland, Mal Meninga seems to enjoy a profile somewhere between the prime minister (and that changed from Ms Gillard to Mr Rudd while we were in the country) and Dame Edna Everage. At least the news pages contained a story about the hotels of Brisbane being full, illustrated with a photo of an engineer and a postman from Wales clinking glasses. They were two of many. The Welsh are amazing. While numbers from other Home Unions grew as the series progressed, Surfers Paradise – where a lot of visitors stayed, our group included – was dominated by men and women in red tops, many of them with accents from west of the Loughor bridge (for the uninitiated, that is by Swansea).

We had a 'Stradey Six', who were admirable examples of the enthusiasm, energy, knowledge and sheer rugby culture of the Lions. Their passion ('pash-un') is something to behold. No surprise really, when one remembers some of the great Lions names hail from Carmarthenshire and nearby: R.H. Williams, Delme, Gerald, Barry, Gareth, Benny and the underrated Stephen Jones; and, of course, Carwyn. Jonathan Davies was their man this time.

Our first night took us to Surfers RFC, who had an old players' match against neighbouring Burleigh Heads RFC. The welcome at their clubhouse was illustrative of the joys of rugby touring anywhere in the world. Drinks were thrust into our hands, and boots of different sizes were produced as the home side were two players short. At a mere 23, Dan Sayers is some way short of veteran status, but his willing participation was a thrill to visitors and hosts alike. At closing time, we left with new friendships made, and a few ideas for the days to come.

Big-match day is different. There is a tingle in the air, a real sense of anticipation. The mood is helped by it being shorts and T-shirt weather. We did a city tour including The Gabba (sports fans just seem to like visiting other sports stadia) and featuring areas along the Brisbane River which suffered badly in the 2011 floods. Our afternoon involved a long lunch at Brothers RFC, where former Wallaby hooker Sean Hardman – a former team-mate of McCall, Eales and Horan – shared his views on the

*ABOVE* The veterans of the Surfers and Burleigh Heads clubs with Lions supporters after their own curtain-raiser to the first Test.

*FACING PAGE* A view of Queensland's Gold Coast.

*BELOW* Brisbane's Caxton Street, bustling on match night.

non-selection of Quade Cooper, and a few amusing stories about Wendell Sailor and Eddie Jones.

And so to Suncorp Stadium. Nearby Caxton Street was reminiscent of Cardiff's Queen Street or the Murrayfield Hotel on international day, except the warm early evening was more conducive to open-air prediction and speculation than a Six Nations fixture. The Test was close and exciting, and afterwards we commiserated with opposition supporters, conceding their extensive injuries meant they had been unlucky to lose.

With only a few days up north, the trip had been fairly hectic so far. Down in Melbourne, surely the pace would slacken off somewhat. Would it heck! The Rebels game was an interesting interlude on a chilly evening, but merely served to underline the gulf that has opened between provincial and Test matches now. Tours of the MCG and the Rod Laver Arena provided pre-match entertainment, as did refreshments in the famous Young and Jacksons bar opposite the Flinders Street station. There we ran into Sean Holley and Shane Williams (a recent Ospreys coach, and an even more recent Lions wing), who led the community singing with a brand-new guitar, already bearing Lions signatures and later to be auctioned.

Thursday was a trip down the Great Ocean Road, and included a lovely moment when one small ageing Welshman saw another walking towards him: 'Oh, my wife saw your wife in the village in the week. She told me you were here.' On Friday night, Roger Baird and John O'Driscoll, both Lions of '83 vintage, kindly did a question and answer session with our group. Both had firm views on certain directions the Lions concept is taking, with which they felt unhappy.

The day of the second Test was yet another which did not require anything more than springtime clothing back in the UK. Like Suncorp, the Etihad Stadium was right downtown, providing easy access following all-day 'preparation'. The Lions performance that evening was rather more sobering, and while most of the tour group wanted a series win at 2-0, the tour leader was quietly pleased with a home win, as it ideally set up the final week in Sydney.

The first part of Sunday was spent at Melbourne RFC, near the Albert Park racetrack. Hong Kong RFC, despite bringing a full first-team squad, could only field ten

— DHL AUSTRALIA —
2013 LIONS TOUR

**Qantas Wallabies**
**v**
**British & Irish Lions**

**Saturday 22 June 2013,**
**Suncorp Stadium**

**TOP** The neon lights of Suncorp Stadium welcome supporters on the first night of the 2013 Wallabies v British & Irish Lions series.

**CENTRE** The match programme for the first Test between Australia and the 2013 Lions.

**LEFT** The pre-match festivities are under way as the series kick-off approaches.

players; it had been a long night. A few of our crew took in an Aussie Rules game at the MCG. In an echo of the 'Sunday school' indulged in by Lions players of yesteryear, we spent the evening in a couple of downtown hostelries, finishing with a lengthy Celtic sing-song led by the president of Machen RFC.

The tour leader was somewhat exhausted as he took Monday's 'red-eye' flight to Sydney, but on emerging from Wynyard train station within sight of the famous Harbour Bridge and Opera House, his spirits lifted upon seeing this special city. Surely the frantic pace of Melbourne would calm? Nope, it increased.

It is a pity that modern itineraries do not include a last midweek game before the final Test. With a huge captive audience in town, it would be nice to have some sort of low-key fixture, maybe for an injured players' charity. No matter, if Jack cannot fill a week in Sydney, then he is a very dull boy indeed. Bridge climbs, harbour tours, the Coogee to Bondi walk, an Opera House visit (including, in the case of Mark Sayers – last year's president of the WRU Referees – actually taking in a Verdi work) and a trip into the Blue Mountains provided ample distraction.

Our popular watering hole was The Rugby Club close to Circular Quay and the harbour. On the Thursday night, so good was the mood, several of those who had tickets for the Old Wallabies v Old Lions game stayed put. The Manic Street Preachers were in town, and James Dean Bradfield graced us with his presence there on Friday night. What a nice man, a clever fellow and a hard-core sports fan; he fitted in well. After the Test, Saturday night became Sunday morning there, and it was close to dawn when the survivors rolled in.

The night of the third Test will live long in the memory. Australia were clear favourites, and optimism was not abundant on the train journey out from Central Station to the Olympic Stadium. The power and pace and ambition of the Lions performance eventually blew the Wallabies away, and set the mood for the 'mother of all celebrations'. The wide smiles spread across thousands of faces atop red shirts told their own stories: 'We are so pleased to have been here to see that.'

An unexpected pleasure of a Lions tour is the old friends one meets by chance. On a single night, I ran into friends from Ulster, South Wales and London, none of whom I knew would be there. That is one of many reasons why you, good reader, should consider doing one.

In case the opening sentiment may be considered hyperbole, I was far from being alone in thinking it. Stuart, a retired open-side from Melton Mowbray RFC, concluded: 'That was the best four days of my life.' He only came for the final Test, yet managed to cram a fortnight's entertainment into that short window. The text he sent me at 6pm on the final Sunday read: 'Am drinking with the Lions at Bondi.'

How many sports offer that? See you in 2017.

*David Stewart was in Australia as a tour leader with All Sports Travel (a sister company to Howzat Travel, in Melton Mowbray, Leicestershire).*

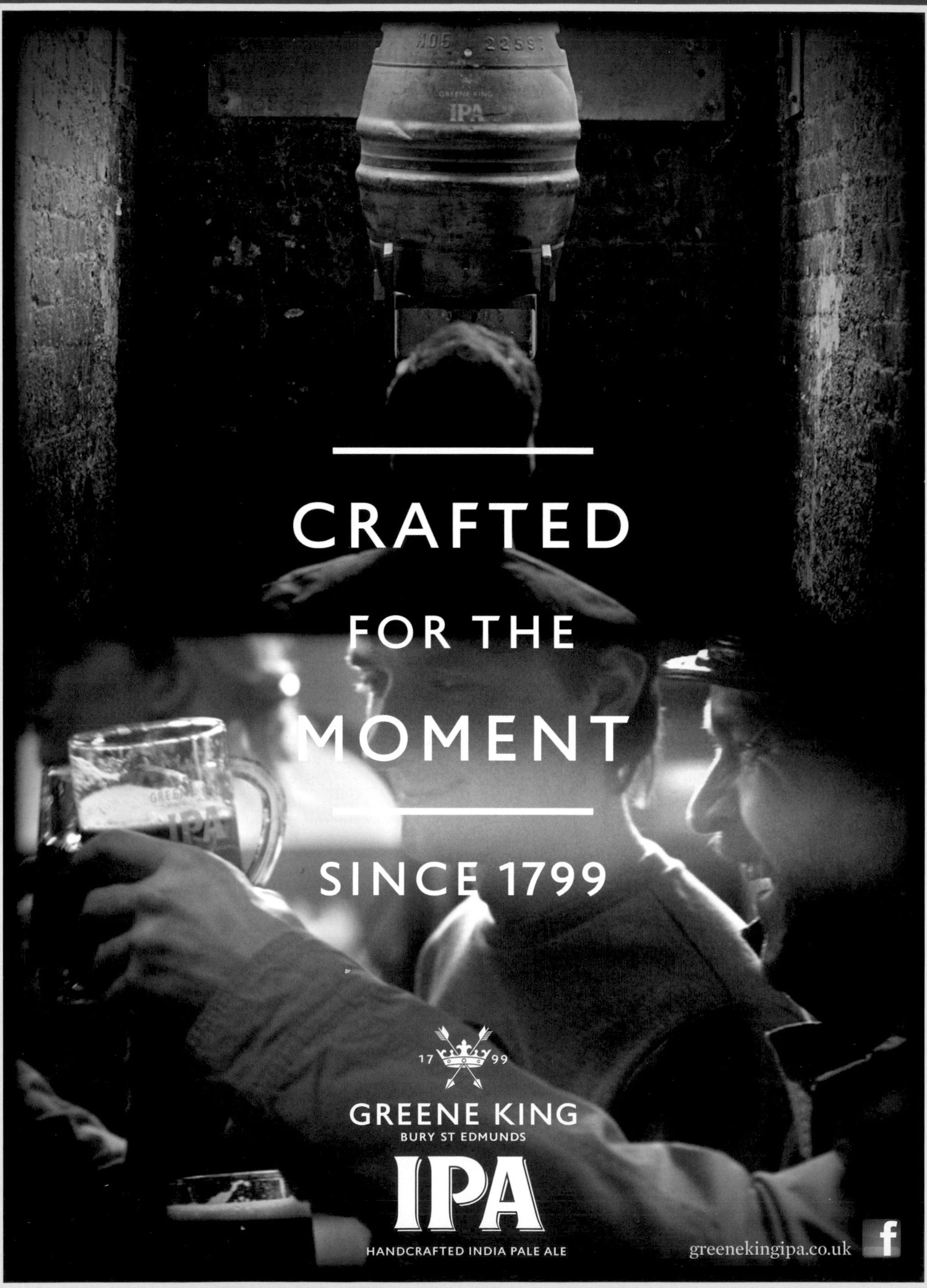

CRAFTED
FOR THE
MOMENT
SINCE 1799
17 99
GREENE KING
BURY ST EDMUNDS
IPA
HANDCRAFTED INDIA PALE ALE
greenekingipa.co.uk

# Mr Versatile
## the Three-Code Career of Israel Folau
### by RAECHELLE INMAN

'He has joined Australia's oldest rugby club, Sydney University, and has made the commitment to provide a scholarship for a young rugby player and student'

It was a stunning debut; one of the most impressive in the history of rugby. Israel Folau had only played 14 rugby (union) matches in his life, all of which were for the New South Wales Waratahs in the Super 15.

The 24-year-old Australian of Tongan descent was thrust into one of the toughest cauldrons: a Test match against the British & Irish Lions. Dubbed one of the finest sportsmen in Australia, he lived up to the hype immediately. It took him just 13 minutes to make a significant impact, capably scoring a try off Will Genia's creativity. He then bagged a double in the 35th minute, easily beating three defenders with a step, fend and pace in a scintillating 40-metre run to the line.

**ABOVE** A debut to remember. Israel Folau strides away from Jonny Sexton and Alex Corbisiero to score his second try for the Wallabies in the first Test against the 2013 Lions.

'It was a fairy-tale debut. I couldn't have asked for a better entry into my international rugby career,' said the shy winger.

Folau also added value in the first Test when he denied Lions winger George North a critical first-half try. 'During that period of time within the circumstances of the game it was lucky that there was no try or the scoreline would have blown out a bit and we would have been chasing our tails. It was a crucial moment but in the end we didn't get the result in that game,' he said.

'The Lions tour is one of the best experiences I have had throughout my football career so far, it

was huge. I didn't think I would be a part of it at the start of the season when I joined the Waratahs but Robbie Deans and the coaching staff gave me an opportunity to be part of it. I was really happy and proud of the way it all turned out, even though the result wasn't what we wanted. Overall it was a great experience.'

So what made is so great? 'Definitely the atmosphere, the Lions fans are so passionate that throughout the games as a player it doesn't matter if they're there for you or you're the opposition player, it gives you a big buzz. That's how I felt throughout the whole series – the atmosphere was great and playing against quality players from four different nations combined was something pretty special.

'My opposing player George North was a stand-out player and being given the chance to play against Brian O'Driscoll, who has been around for a long time, was an awesome experience.

'I have played in big games in rugby league with State of Origin and playing for Australia. Playing State of Origin is an amazing experience with the atmosphere and crowd. But it's different. With the Lions, the supporters sing songs and chant throughout the game, which is something you wouldn't get in an Origin game but the atmosphere is electric at both.'

After Folau's first outing for the Wallabies his team-mate Will Genia described him as 'an absolute freak'.

'We talked him up all week and he came out and proved it. He's a big game player, he's used to playing on the big stage and he delivered.

'We are lucky he is on our side,' said Genia.

Wallaby coach Robbie Deans gave Folau a go despite his complete lack of international experience in rugby and his decision paid quick dividends. 'When you're as well-equipped as he is, he has a lot of confidence to do the things that he does,' Deans said.

'He has a real physical stature so he's not intimidated, he's got fast feet, he's quick, he's got a great offload … it slows the defence down because they're conscious of all the options, and he is very good at taking the options.'

Folau has a history as a prolific try scorer. In his first 14 games for the Waratahs, he scored eight tries, and at the elite level in rugby league he impressed, with five in seven games for Australia, five in five games for Queensland, 37 in 38 games for Brisbane, and 36 in 52 games for Melbourne Storm.

He was just 17 when he made his debut in the 2007 National Rugby League (NRL) season, the youngest player to represent the Melbourne Storm. In his rookie year he broke a number of club and NRL records, including the NRL record for most tries in a season. In 2007 he also became the youngest ever to play for the Kangaroos, the Australian rugby league team. The following year he became the youngest player to represent Queensland in the State of Origin. He moved from the Melbourne Storm to the Brisbane Broncos in 2009 before the lure of one of the highest salaries in Australian sport and a new challenge saw him cross codes to the Australian Football League (AFL) in 2011.

In 2012 Folau made his AFL debut in the Greater Western Sydney Giants first match in the senior national AFL competition, against the Sydney Swans. Folau brought profile to the game of Aussie Rules in Sydney's Western suburbs, a traditional stronghold of rugby league.

'Kicking in AFL helped me a lot … it also taught me a lot and little things such as being aware and making quick decisions as this is a big part of AFL … so that has helped me in rugby as well. And different skills like transferring the ball through my hands has also helped.'

*FACING PAGE* Claiming the high ball. Folau shows his aerial skills during the Waratahs captain's run ahead of round three of Super Rugby 2013.

*BELOW* Israel Folau demonstrates the defensive aspect of his game, denying George North a try at a crucial point in the first Lions Test.

Folau showcased the aerial skills, leap and the accurate kicking game he learned from AFL in his first season in rugby. His coach at the Giants was AFL legend Kevin Sheedy, who describes Folau as the ultimate prototype for contact sports. 'Kevin Sheedy has been really supportive, even when I left the Giants,' said the code hopper.

'I've been fortunate to have some great coaches throughout my career. When I played league for the Storm in Melbourne Craig Bellamy was a big influence on my career. With rugby I've had Michael Cheika and Robbie Deans, with the time I've had to work with Robbie he has been exceptional and I'm a bit sad he's not going to be the coach for the Wallabies but that's not within my control,' he continued.

Combining his new-found AFL skills and finesse, balanced with his innate power, strength and speed, set him in good stead to 'hit the ground running' on the international rugby stage. 'Rugby is played around the world whereas league and AFL are a lot more central to Australia. That's the big difference for me … it's great that rugby is a global game, so to get the opportunity to travel around the world to countries I wouldn't usually go to is what I love about it. I look forward to doing it a lot more.'

Rugby is a very technical game and Folau admits he still hasn't mastered all of the rules. 'I still have a lot to learn and a lot to improve on my game … in defence there's still a lot to learn when I go into the ruck and the breakdown. Overall I have been happy with my progress in my first year so far but there's still a lot for me to learn in defence and attack, I feel like I can inject myself a lot more in attack with the ball.'

That's an ominous warning from one of the most complete players the world has seen. If his confidence in rugby continues to grow and he really unleashes, the impact for the opposition will be devastating. His versatility is also an advantage to any side he plays for, having already shown he is adept on the wing or at full back; he would like to play in the centres to ensure he gets more ball.

'I love the culture of rugby; the people who are involved in the organisation are very professional.

'I dreamed about being a Kangaroo [Australian rugby league representative] when I grew up but my parents are from the Islands, so rugby is a bigger game where they're from. I watched rugby as a little kid but never did I think I would put on a Wallabies jersey when I was young … but the way the journey has turned out, it has been amazing.

'I have a lot of family back in Tonga and they support and watch my games and I try to get back there at Christmas time if I can for a week or two.'

Folau is a religious young man and goes to a small Christian church for a Tongan service every Sunday and helps out there when he can. He has joined Australia's oldest rugby club, Sydney University, and has made the commitment to provide a scholarship for a young rugby player and student: the 'Israel Folau Scholarship'.

'I want to put back into the community and one way to do it was to give one Tongan kid an opportunity to play rugby or even if he didn't want to play rugby to study and pursue a career. I was happy to do that.'

He is well aware of his Tongan roots, his church and his family values. He also credits his close-knit family as the driving force behind his sporting success. 'My family motivates me to get up each day, to get up and go and try to be the best I can, and also for my own personal benefits … as a young kid that's all I wanted to do, to be a professional footballer and I want to help myself.

'I'm very close to my family. I'm a pretty relaxed guy, outside of rugby I hang out with my close mates and go for a feed or watch a movie; I also love going to the beach and just chilling out. I'm pretty "cruisy". My mates would describe me as relaxed; a cool and calm operator.'

What would his sister Mary say about him? 'I'm a bit shy and quiet, she would say I need to talk and open up a bit more.'

And with all the attention on Folau he will slowly have to become more comfortable with that. For now he is weighing up options for his future, with a bidding war between league and union a likely scenario.

'I'd love to stay in rugby, I've been enjoying it. I'd love to be part of the World Cup.'

Let's hope Australian rugby holds onto this valuable asset to the code.

**FACING PAGE** 'A cool and calm operator' – Israel Folau in relaxed mood during Wallabies training, August 2013.

next

# INTERNATIONAL SCENE

# Brothers in Rugby
## the Kaplans of Israel

### by CHRIS THAU

'The fact that both my boys play the game with such passion means a lot to me. I am really happy that I succeeded in passing on the love for the game to them'

Watching his country winning all their matches in division 2B of the FIRA-AER Championship has given former Israel captain Milton Kaplan a genuine sense of fulfilment. And this is not only because the team he captained in a pioneering tour abroad in 1981 has made such spectacular progress – climbing in five years no less than 43 places in the IRB rankings – but also because his two sons, Yonatan and Nimrod, are such a big part of it. Born in South Africa in 1948, Milton, nowadays a dairy farmer in Kibbutz Yizreel, commenced playing at the age of nine on the hard gravel fields of Winburg, in the Orange Free State.

'Rugby has always been a big part in our family. My father Boris Kaplan played for Winburg club before World War II and during the war he had the honour of captaining the South African Army team against the Air Force. The match was played in Pretoria and that was the first ever win of the Army against the Air Force. After the war, when he returned to civilian life he took up refereeing and that is when I got involved in the game. When I arrived in Israel in 1973 rugby was in its infancy so I started playing with my fellow workers at Kibbutz Yizreel on a patch of grass, after it was cut to feed the cows,' he recalled.

It was another South African, Leo Camron, a Natal University graduate and Israeli Army officer, who organised the first rugby match between a team of South African immigrants and a team of paratroopers in 1952 – though it has to be said that rugby had been played in the country during the British mandate. 'To help the spectators understand what went on we had leaflets with the Laws of the Game translated into Hebrew, which got distributed before the match,' recalled Camron, who also started cricket in Israel. The South Africans won 18-6, but unfortunately the Army top brass did not share the enthusiasm for rugby of Camron and his paratroopers and banned it.

*ABOVE* Nimrod Kaplan (centre) playing for his club, Kibbutz Yizreel.

*FACING PAGE* The rugby-playing Kaplans. Milton flanked by sons Nimrod (left) and Yonatan.

By the time Kaplan arrived in Israel, rugby had been revived by a group of South African students at Tel Aviv University, followed by the formation of the Israeli Rugby Union in 1971. The formation, by the mainly South African farmers, of Kibbutz Yizreel rugby club, to date one of the main strongholds of the game in the country, provided the students with tough opposition. Soon the game spread to other universities and by the mid-1970s a fledgling league was operational. The first tourists were a British Army team from Cyprus in 1972, with the newly formed Israeli team winning its first international engagement 14-12. The thirst for international competition was partially quenched by the visiting South African teams, unfortunately far too strong for the raw Israeli opposition.

Milton Kaplan recalls: 'In 1974-75 Northern Transvaal, who had won the Currie Cup that year were sent on a goodwill tour of Israel and Europe. There were six Springboks in the side so beating them was not on the cards. They scored over 70 points and I remember the father of the present captain of the Blue Bulls Pierre Spies running in six tries. Most of the teams that came to play against us were too strong and hence we lost continuously. However, the strong camaraderie that existed between the players from all over the country kept us going.'

'The tour to France and Switzerland in 1981 started a new era of rugby in Israel. We became a member of FIRA and started building bridges with Europe. I had the honour of captaining the team on our first official tour, when we played our first Test against Switzerland. We drew 9-all in the pouring rain in Geneva. It was a memorable moment in our history,' Milton Kaplan added.

With their father as coach, mentor and role model, it is not surprising that both sons – Yonatan, a bony 6ft 6in lock forward, and Nimrod, a 6ft 3in No. 8-cum-centre – found rugby irresistible, though Nimrod tried soccer, basketball and swimming before making rugby his favourite sport. Now both of them are seasoned internationals with more than 20 caps under their belts and both, in another twist of fate, followed in their father's footsteps to become captains of their country. If Milton Kaplan captained Israel in their maiden international in 1981, Yonatan became the sixth Israel captain 20 years later in 2001, while brother Nimrod took over as skipper in 2010, before Yonatan returned this year.

'It's a huge honour to captain your country. I started playing during our "darker years" when we lost far more than we won and to be part of this transition is very satisfying. Now with my better years behind me I am privileged to be in a position that I can mentor younger players and develop a positive rugby environment. As I got older, there has always been the weight of expectation to follow into my dad's footsteps and I happily embraced it. There is nothing more gratifying for me than to meet an ex-player that played with him or who was coached by him and to hear the amount of respect and admiration they have for him. If it was not for him and his friends rugby could have easily vanished from the Israeli scene,' Yonatan said.

Yonatan, now in his second stint as Israel captain, started his international career at the age of 19 as No. 8 and skipper of a successful Israeli Youth team in a FIRA Under 19 tournament in Lausanne in 1999. A week later he made his international debut for the senior side, in a rather traumatic 40-7 defeat at the hands of Switzerland. The following year he honed his skills in France playing for the Reichel Juniors (Under 20) of the ASVEL club in Villeurbanne, near Lyons, with whom he reached the final of the French Championship, only to lose to Pau in the final. In March 2001 he was appointed captain of the national team for the match against Luxembourg, but at the end of the 2002 season, left after only eight matches in charge to join the Army. In 2004, after National Service, he went to New York, where he joined the Old Blue club, being picked twice for the North East Select XV in the USA All Star tournament. He made a brief return in 2008, when he and Nimrod appeared together for Israel for the first time, in a crucial relegation match against Cyprus.

'The fact that both my boys play the game with such passion means a lot to me. I am really happy that I succeeded in passing on the love for the game to them,' observed Milton.

'Yonatan, from a very young age developed a passion for rugby. He could sit for hours in front of the TV watching a game. Physically he was always big and strong so he could hold his own on the rugby field, even against those older than him. Nimrod had to work harder at his game. It was clear that he would follow the same path as Yonatan and would go to France after school. After a season in France he went to Australia, where he joined the Randwick club, then after his Army service Nimrod spent two years in London playing for London Scottish. Both Bernice and me are proud of our boys and their contribution to the game on and off the field,' Milton Kaplan said.

During Yonatan's absence, his younger brother made his international debut against Lithuania in 2004. This was the kind of 50-point disaster Israel were prone to during the early part of the decade. The turning point, recalled Nimrod, was the relegation 'do or die' match against Cyprus in September 2008, for which several of the experienced regulars, including the two brothers, at the time playing abroad, returned home.

'This was at a time of major changes at the Israeli Rugby Union Board with Menachem Ben Menachem elected president and Raanan Penn appointed head coach. Both the players and the IRU Board understood this is a must win match, and changes had to be made. At the same time the players playing abroad (Matan Brosh, Yonatan and myself) we were asked to come over to make sure Israel win this match. The final score was 23-14 for Israel. The whole team enjoyed the winning feeling after so many losses before. From that point onwards, the attitudes changed and both players and staff started to put much more effort in the team and did all it takes to win more matches,' recalled Nimrod Kaplan, who took over as captain against Bulgaria in 2010.

In a country where miracles are not that infrequent, the recent campaign of the Israeli team in the FIRA-AER Championship, which ended with an emphatic seven-try 46-3 win over an ambitious, yet limited, Denmark, could only be described as a minor miracle. It was the Israeli front five of Nathan Amos, Oren Alt, Matan Brosh, Oren Brodhurst and Yonatan Kaplan who did most of the damage, ably supported by a marauding back row of Julien Maffi, Guy Matisis and Michael Eli at No. 8 – with the younger Nimrod Kaplan sidelined by injury. To add to the Danish woes, the Israeli line out, accurately served by hooker and former skipper Oren Alt (at 42, probably the oldest international player in the qualifying rounds of RWC 2015) worked a treat, with captain Kaplan making an outstanding contribution, until he ran out of juice towards the end of the match.

Israeli Union president Menachem Ben Menachem, a former international flank forward in the early 1990s, does not believe in miracles and argues that the input of the new coach Raanan Penn, another former captain of the national side, as well as a change of players' attitude are the key ingredients of the Israeli revival.

'There is no miracle really. This is the progress of a talented side with an experienced pack of forwards and some gifted fleet-footed youngsters. Penn's input was huge but he benefited from a change in attitude of the players. They are all amateurs, but they train like professionals. Since the game became an Olympic sport we benefit from the support of the Israeli Olympic Committee which makes a big difference,' Mr Ben Menachem said.

'I think our last game against Denmark, which I captained, was probably our best ever performance,' added Yonatan Kaplan. 'We dominated the collision area and executed the game plan to perfection. Of course, the ultimate dream would be for Israel to make the Olympic Games or/and the World Cup, but this is not realistic. If rugby can grow the same way in the next 15 years the way it has progressed in the past 15, I would be very happy.'

To cap a remarkably successful season, the Israel team, captained by Yonatan Kaplan, won the gold medal in the Maccabiah Games, the quadrennial Jewish Olympics, for the first time ever, defeating the Australian team, the previous holders, 13-0 in the final at the end of July.

> **BELOW** Israel skipper Yonatan Kaplan (left) and his second-row partner Oren Brodhurst congratulate scrum half Eitan Humphreys on his try against Denmark in Netanya.

# The Wheel Turns
## the 2013 Junior World Championship
### by ALAN LORIMER

'If there was an element of fortune in England having USA in their pool, then there was nothing owed to luck about their semi-final performance against New Zealand'

Northern-hemisphere rugby has for too long been the kicking boy of the IRB Junior World Championship, ruled until last year by New Zealand and then taken over by South Africa. But in 2013 the old order took a severe bashing as England and Wales fought out the first ever northern-hemisphere final at the Stade de la Rabine in Vannes, from which the reigning Under 20s Six Nations champions, England, emerged winners.

Not that there was any surprise that England should have reached the final. The men in white contested the inaugural Under 20 championship final, staged in Wales, but lost heavily, 38-3, to New Zealand. A year later, in Japan, England got closer but had to settle for a 44-28 defeat to the Baby Blacks. England's best chance for the title appeared to be in 2011, when in Padova New Zealand had to come from

**BELOW** England Under 20 skipper Jack Clifford and his team with the JWC trophy.

behind before taking the honours with a 33-22 win. A blip followed last year in South Africa, when England finished seventh, but their form in the Under 20s Six Nations and the appointment of a new head coach in Nick Walshe signalled potential success in the World Juniors.

Yet in the pool stages not everyone would have bet on England. Walshe's side lost narrowly to South Africa but had a comfortable win over France, albeit without garnering a four-try bonus point. That left England with five championship points with one pool match to play. Fortunately their opponents were USA, who had already revealed their rawness by losing 97-0 to South Africa and 45-3 to France.

Against the amateurs of USA, England's young professionals simply ran amok, winning 109-0 to finish their pool stage with ten points, the same as Ireland and Argentina. But the USA factor massively skewed the points-difference table in favour of England and it was to the semi-finals that Walshe's charges were able to advance.

If there was an element of fortune in England having USA in their pool, then there was nothing owed to luck about their semi-final performance against New Zealand. England led 23-8 eleven minutes into the second half, with three penalties from Henry Slade and the fly half's conversions of tries by flanker Matt Hankin and winger Anthony Watson. But New Zealand then showed typical fighting spirit to bring the score back to 23-21, before England took a grip of the game in the final minutes to score through replacement prop Tom Smallbone; Slade added the conversion and then a penalty to make sure of England's place in the final.

For Wales the Junior World Championship was all about building on their excellent showing in the 2012 tournament in South Africa, when the Welshmen produced a shock defeat of New Zealand in the pool stages before losing to the Baby Blacks in the semi-finals.

Wales, runners-up in the 2013 Under 20s Six Nations, looked committed from the outset, winning Pool C with victories over Samoa, Scotland and Argentina to book their place in the semi-final against Pool A winners South Africa.

If the organisers had wanted an advert for Junior World Championship rugby, then they would not have found any better than the Wales v South Africa semi-final. The Baby Boks, having scored a try through lock Irne Herbst – which was converted by Handre Pollard, the only survivor from South Africa's winning team last year – led 7-6 at the break, only for Wales's captain Ellis Jenkins to put his side ahead 11-7 with an unconverted try.

The pendulum then swung in favour of South Africa as replacement flanker Kwagga Smith crossed for a try converted by Pollard, who then added a penalty goal for a 17-11 advantage. It looked all over for Wales until two minutes from full-time, when their mercurial full back Jordan Williams set off on a run, his sidestep leaving South African defenders clutching at air before he was finally brought to ground. When Wales recycled the ball, fly half Sam Davies showed vision of an exceptional calibre, spotting space in the right-hand corner and putting in a delicate chip that allowed winger Ashley Evans to gather and score. 17-16 for South Africa and a touch-line conversion to follow. Davies made no mistake with the kick, giving Wales victory and a place in the final.

And so to the final. Could Wales repeat their success against South Africa? It certainly looked propitious when Wales moved into a 15-3 lead with two tries from Ashley Evans and a penalty and conversion from Davies. Just before half-time England appeared to make inroads when Leicester lock Dominic Barrow touched down. But the big second-row was adjudged to have engaged in foul play moments earlier – a yellow card ensued and the 'try' was chalked off. That should have been a further advantage for Wales, but instead it was 14-man England who gradually took control of the game, their more powerful pack and an enviably strong bench being critical factors. Tries by full back Jack Nowell and chunky centre Sam Hill, both converted by Henry Slade, gave England a 17-15 lead, and when fly half Slade kicked two late penalty goals it was England's title.

England won the championship because they had professional power throughout their squad that allowed the coaching team to rotate their players, and because there was an element of luck in drawing USA in their group. They did too have some top-class individual performers, notably their dynamic No. 8 and skipper Jack Clifford and front-row Luke Cowan-Dickie.

Wales lacked the overall strength that England possessed, but in fly half Sam Davies, voted IRB Junior Player of the Year, full back Jordan Williams, scrum half Rhodri Williams and flanker Ellis Jenkins they have players who will surely advance to senior level.

Aberdeen Asset Management is proud to support Wooden Spoon and wish them every success in all their upcoming events.

The value of investments, and the income from them, may go down as well as up and you may get back less than the amount invested.

For more information please visit:
**aberdeen-asset.com/sponsorship**

Simply asset management.

Like Wales, New Zealand had a number of talented players, not least their captain and Sevens representative Ardie Savea, lock Patrick Tuipulotu, centre Michael Collins and fly half Simon Hickey. For South Africa, winger Seabelo Senatla, another Sevens representative, emerged as a star, as did skipper Ruan Steenkamp.

South Africa gained some solace for their semi-final defeat by finishing third after defeating New Zealand 41-34, while in the fifth/sixth play-off France finally came good to achieve a 37-34 victory over Argentina. In seventh place were Australia, who defeated Ireland 28-17, a disappointing ending for the Irish, who had beaten the young Wallabies in the pool stage and run New Zealand very close.

In the bottom group of countries (places nine to 12), it was Samoa who finished top of the heap after the powerful Pacific Islanders defeated close rivals Fiji in the fourth round and then Scotland in the final match. For Scotland the difficult truth is that squads need to be totally professional to compete at this level otherwise they risk being overpowered. The Scots, however, can be happy that a number of players, including centre Mark Bennett, fly half Tommy Allan, winger Damien Hoyland, back-row Adam Ashe and lock Jonny Gray, emerged as stars. But without a powerhouse front row the Scots were always going to struggle, in which context they will be annoyed that they allowed Scott Wilson to emigrate south and play for England.

USA will return to the second tier and Italy will rejoin the elite group for the 2014 Junior World Championship being staged in Auckland. That will provide the perfect opportunity for New Zealand to reclaim top spot, but with England and Wales having tasted success this year, northern-hemisphere confidence should be high.

**BELOW** Full back Jack Nowell scores England's first try of the final against Wales.

# Back to the Future
## the Brumbies Under Jake White
### by RAECHELLE INMAN

'Talking to White, the word "non-negotiable" recurs. He has rigorous standards and one gets the feeling any breaches of these standards would not be tolerated'

When Jake White, a 48-year-old South African World Cup-winning coach, took over as coach of the Brumbies Super 15 side at the end of 2011 he said: 'The most important thing was to get back to the things that were most important for the Brumbies so we adopted the slogan "Back to the Future".'

This was a clever approach from a smart man.

The Brumbies were an exceptional provincial side in the early days of Super Rugby. Australia's capital had no history of rugby union. In the 1990s a side was famously created by throwing together players who had been discarded from the established provinces of New South Wales and Queensland. A few Canberra lads were thrown into the pot to give it some local flavour. The players were all from somewhere else and so these Brumbies mostly lived together in the one apartment block – nicknamed 'Melrose Place'. They had an innovative coach in Rod Macqueen, and their story was the fairy tale of Australian rugby. The so-called 'outcasts' developed a strong culture as an incredibly tightknit group of mates, irreverently taking the challenge to the established rugby provinces, and created a selfless rugby side that dazzled on the field.

Between 2000 and 2004 they won two Super Rugby titles and made the finals every year. Those five years were the glory days, but then they lost their way and White was just the man to bring them back. It was an era that White was quick to focus on emulating. In doing so, he made an astute emotional connection for the people of Canberra, a small city where the locals are passionate about their teams. The fans craved a return to the winning ways of the Brumbies, a time when their culture was second to none, a period stamped by a contagious and humble self-belief.

White inherited a struggling side that finished the 2011 Super 15 series in lowly thirteenth place. His focused approach has moved them up the rankings so that in 2013 they secured the Australian conference and made the Super Rugby final for the first time in nine years. The Canberra side looked like they would win the championship, dominating for 60 minutes in Hamilton, before the Chiefs stole a come-from-behind victory, 27-22.

Perhaps even more importantly for sentiment and establishing their presence on the global stage, in near freezing conditions the Brumbies achieved a historic win over the British & Irish Lions: the only provincial side to achieve this feat on the 2013 tour and only the fourth Australian non-national team ever to achieve it after Queensland in 1971 and New South Wales in 1950 and 1959.

Some say that the British & Irish Lions were a second-string side, but when you consider the team is drawn from all the Home Nations and that the Brumbies were without 11 of their usual starting line-up who were on Australian duty, it remains a remarkable achievement.

The master coach counted the 14-12 upset amongst the most satisfying in his career and it looks even more impressive when you consider the Wallabies only won one of their three games (and by a

**ABOVE** Brumbies prop Scott Sio has a dart during the 2013 Super Rugby final in Hamilton, in which the Canberra outfit had the upper hand until a last-quarter burst from the Chiefs nicked a 27-22 win.

**FACING PAGE** A happy Jake White after his Brumbies had defeated the 2013 British & Irish Lions in Canberra.

**PAGE 42** Flanker Scott Fardy gets the better of Billy Twelvetrees as the Brumbies become the only provincial side to beat the 2013 Lions.

smaller margin!). 'I've been lucky enough to win a senior and junior World Cup, but to beat the Lions, especially the way it was done, with a group of boys with 28 Test caps, of which one player [Clyde Rathbone] has 26, and another [skipper Peter Kimlin] two.

'It's got to be as good as it gets in rugby union.'

For White, taking on the challenge of the Brumbies was perfect timing.

'I wanted to get back into coaching and I was trying to find the right job in terms of where I thought I could add value; but, also where I could go to a franchise or a club or a team that would suit the way I wanted to coach … I had also always enjoyed the way the Brumbies played and I wanted to get back into an environment where you basically get a blank piece of paper,' he said.

The man who took the Springboks to victory in the 2007 Rugby World Cup went into the role with a profound respect for the province.

'It was exciting because I knew how massive the Brumbies brand was in South Africa … some of the great players who played for Australia and the Brumbies are well known in South Africa and I thought that it would be a great time to re-visit all the things that were good for the Brumbies and also add something new that would create a new legacy with this group,' White enthused.

'From outside a lot of people had spoken about how [in the past] the Brumbies players all lived together and could talk rugby and come up with new ideas because of the fact that they spent so much time together and so that excited me because I have always thought that is one of the non-negotiables in getting successful teams together; the environment you can create and the togetherness you can create on and off the rugby field.

'It's a unique situation in Canberra, it's a small town and everyone can get together, there are not too many distractions. You come here because you take your rugby seriously – there's no Bondi, there's no flashing lights like the big cities but if you are serious about rugby and giving yourself a fair crack at making it we can offer you the best we can in making sure you get everything you need to make it as a rugby player.

'We have had 160 boys play for the Brumbies since 1996 and we have had over 80 play for the Wallabies, which means that one in every two becomes a Wallaby. There aren't many franchises in world sport that give you a 50 per cent chance of playing for your country. It's something that the Brumbies are very proud of and it is the greatness of having that as a track record for young boys to understand that if you really want to make it and you're really dedicated there's no reason why you can't use the Brumbies to play at a high level.'

White quickly restructured the programme in Canberra and immediately saw the value that local favourite son and former Wallaby great Stephen Larkham would bring to the table as a coach of the backs. 'Stephen is one of the most humble rugby players you will ever meet in your life, he is a household name yet the way he walks around as if he's never played rugby yet he's played more than 100 times for Australia and he's done everything you can in rugby union. There's no doubt that having him, his attitude, how he perceives things, how he talks about and how he conducts himself is definitely important for this young group of players to look up to not only as player but as a person who doesn't act like he is owed anything in rugby.'

Along with Larkham and other key support staff, White began to build a winning culture headlined by some good old-fashioned discipline. This approach paid immediate dividends in his first season at the helm, taking the Brumbies from the wilderness to the cusp of the Super Rugby finals in 2012.

'It is non-negotiable rugby discipline and I guess because rugby union is so important and it's number one in South Africa it comes naturally to me to get players to understand that if you're going to do it you might as well do it properly, there's no use doing it half-heartedly and that means expecting certain behaviours and taking responsibility for your actions that's the way it is.'

White talks candidly about players earning significant sums of money and the obligation that comes with that: 'You cannot expect someone to be living the life of a CEO financially – I mean these players earn massive amounts of money – and then act like a Varsity student. Something has got to give and what I try to get them to understand is that if you want the luxuries and to be privy to be a well-paid athlete and spend time doing what you enjoy and getting paid for it that comes at a price and that price is you cannot behave like your mate who is 22 years old and studying at university and gets an allowance and drives a bashed up car and goes out every Friday and Saturday night to spend his money. Players understand that ... if they have to make certain sacrifices along the way and one of those is the way they look after themselves, the way they conduct themselves and obviously have mutual respect for people around them.'

Talking to White, the word 'non-negotiable' recurs. He has rigorous standards and one gets the feeling any breaches of these standards would not be tolerated.

'What you do off the field has a direct impact on what you do on the field, there's no doubt in my mind. If you're disciplined that's what you will do in the game. If you don't have it off the field it's very hard to have structure and organisation and discipline on the field.'

This approach is evident in the lack of ego at the Brumbies: the province has avoided the controversy other Australian teams have suffered due to 'rock star'-like behaviour, with high-profile players like Quade Cooper, Kurtley Beale and James O'Connor topping the list.

Rather than focusing on themselves as 'brands', the humility of the Brumbies has translated into selfless players on the field, a testament to the old adage – 'a champion team, rather than a team of champions'.

'You want players to enjoy what they are doing and that means creating an environment where everyone feels they have worth. It doesn't matter whether it's the baggage master or the physiotherapist or if it's player 35 who probably doesn't even get a game during the season because the team is playing well and there are no injuries so it's about covering all of those bases and making sure they all have some sort of sense of worth in the club.

'You identify that [a selfless approach] as a key area and get players to understand how important that is and as they develop as a squad and they get success and they start to realise that no one is better than anyone else they start to feel their worth in the group then that rubs off on the next person and they start creating that culture and controlling that culture and that is even more important.

'People say we don't have any of those [rock stars] and that's because the group itself don't allow that to happen and that's part of the management role as well, setting the trend and getting them to understand the value and importance of everyone buying in.

'One of the things that's vital to any team is that understanding and belief of being a special team and the closeness of the group.'

The types of players White has recruited such as back-rows David Pocock and Ben Mowen exemplify this philosophy.

'Ben [Mowen] has the ability to bring the best out in guys who are 32 years old in our squad and guys who are 20 years old in our squad and I think that's the uniqueness of his leadership skills, the ability to get through to some of the young guys coming through the professional ranks and the ability to motivate some of the older guys who are near the end of their campaign.

'He has proved himself in Super Rugby as one of the top leaders in the competition. He has had to sacrifice a lot of things, he has [had] to pack up and move away from home. He comes from Brisbane and he then had to go and play for the Waratahs and then he went to the Reds for a while

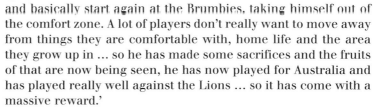

and basically start again at the Brumbies, taking himself out of the comfort zone. A lot of players don't really want to move away from things they are comfortable with, home life and the area they grow up in ... so he has made some sacrifices and the fruits of that are now being seen, he has now played for Australia and has played really well against the Lions ... so it has come with a massive reward.'

White speaks with passion about his players. 'I don't like to single out guys because every guy here puts up their hand and that's what's so nice .... There are no superstars; from blind-side flanker Scott Fardy who's an older guy to Jesse Mogg who's a younger guy. Prop Scott Sio has come from nowhere to Wallaby contention. Lock Peter Kimlin has gone from playing Test rugby many years ago to getting his name called up now.

'That's what's so exciting about coming here ... when you have an impact on how players' rugby careers and lives develop. It's all about understanding that everyone has worth and can contribute.'

White also mentions the word 'worth' regularly; he clearly places huge emphasis on being aware of the value each individual contributes to the franchise and making sure everyone feels a collective sense of community and inclusion.

A member of the coveted IRB Hall of Fame and twice IRB International Coach of the Year, White is somewhat 'old school' and stern. But he is not gruff or ignorant; in fact he presents as very worldly, very smart and also approachable. His style seems to be just what the Brumbies needed.

White's mission is clear and simple: 'We want to create our own legacy but we want to be mindful of what a great legacy and history and benchmark the Brumbies have had in the past.'

*LEFT* Ben Mowen, Brumbies skipper and Wallaby flanker, talks to his team during their Super Rugby round 14 match against the Waratahs at Sydney's ANZ Stadium.

# The Road to England
## RWC 2015 Qualifying Begins

by CHRIS THAU

'It was Madagascar captain José Rakoto Harison and his fellow centre Rija Edmond Rakotoarimanana who stole the show, scoring between them five of the eight tries'

The qualifying process for RWC 2015 commenced on the playing fields of Iberoamericana University in the district of Santa Fe in Mexico City in March 2012, with the Mexican 'Snakes', or Las Serpientes as they call themselves, taking on Jamaica in the North (NACRA) section of the Americas Zone. True to the pre-match promise of the Mexico coach and No. 8, New Zealand-born Simon Pierre, the match was a 'fiesta' of attacking rugby, with the Mexicans running in nine tries to Jamaica's two, for a final scoreline of 68-14. The pre-match pomp and ceremony included a visit from IRB chairman Bernard Lapasset, who brought with him the Webb Ellis Cup and RWC winner Lawrence Dallaglio, who presented the jerseys to the two teams. The match was refereed by South Africa's Craig Joubert, an appointment that reflects the desire of the organisers to present the RWC as a continual process, with Joubert, the referee of the previous RWC final, being in charge of the opening match of the new RWC cycle.

For the record, Mexico full back Pascal Nadaud scored the first try of the new RWC, and outside half Miguel Carner, the son of the founding Mexican Union president, landed both the first

conversion and the first penalty. This was the first of the 184 matches that are to be played in the qualifying rounds of RWC 2015. One month and four NACRA matches later, on 21 April, the favourites Mexico found themselves unceremoniously knocked out 46-13 by the Caymans at the Truman Bodden Stadium in Georgetown. They in turn lost to Bermuda, the eventual winners of the NACRA qualifying round.

In round three Bermuda were pitted against Paraguay, the winners of the South (CONSUR) section of the Americas Zone. Although they benefited in the build-up from some expert advice from former England captain Lewis Moody, Bermuda were knocked out 29-14 by the Paraguayan Yacarés (Crocodiles) at the University of Asunción last September. The win enabled Los Yacarés to challenge arch-rivals Brazil for the coveted fourth slot in the South American Championship alongside Argentina, Uruguay and Chile the following month. They failed, as the Brazilians, coached by Canterbury RFU duo Brent Frew and Scott Robertson, were too hot to handle, winning 35-22 in front of a record 6000 crowd in São Paolo. Currently Brazilian rugby is on a high, having signed a five-year agreement with the Canterbury RFU (New Zealand) and the Crusaders franchise, who will assist the CBRu high-performance programme and the development of the elite Brazilian players until 2017. Furthermore, additional coaching support for Brazilian grass-roots rugby has been offered by England's Aviva Premiership, who in association with the British Council sent 12 young coaches to the country for a year.

With Argentina already qualified for England 2015, the Americas Zone has been allocated two further starting positions (Americas 1 and Americas 2) and one place in the Repechage. Argentina routinely won the four-nation South American Championship, though it was Uruguay, coached by Pablo Lemoine, the country's first professional player, who topped the three-nation RWC 2015 qualifier. They first dealt summarily with Brazil, scoring seven tries in a 58-7 demolition, with both Juan and Agustín Ormaechea, the sons of RWC 1999 captain and RWC 2003 coach Diego, on the scoresheet, and then defeated Chile – always a hard nut to crack – 23-9. That has given Los Teros the right to challenge the losers of the USA v Canada home and away series for the second Americas qualifying position (Americas 2) later on this year. The two-match clash between a resurgent USA and Canada in August provides an intriguing contest for the first Americas entry (Americas 1).

The winners of the rather complicated African qualifying process will join Pool B of RWC 2015 as Africa 1, with the runners-up granted access to the Repechage process. RWC regulars Namibia remain in contention for their fifth RWC appearance, though they were given a fright in the opening round of the Africa Zone, which kicked off with the first division of the African Confederation (CAR), involving Madagascar, Morocco, Namibia and Senegal, in July 2012. This included quite an extraordinary rugby match between hosts Madagascar and Namibia in which 16 tries and over 100 points were scored, with the Malagasy team prevailing narrowly 57-54 in extra time. It was Madagascar captain José Rakoto Harison and his fellow centre Rija Edmond Rakotoarimanana who stole the show, scoring between them five of the eight Madagascar tries and 42 of their 57 points.

In their earlier game against an abrasive and surprisingly competent Senegal, Namibia found themselves trailing by one point with some ten minutes to go and must thank their outside half Theuns Kotze, whose dropped goal just moments before the end secured them the much needed 20-18 win to remain in the race for RWC 2015. A week later in Gaborone, Botswana managed to overtake Côte d'Ivoire, though equal on points, in a tournament disrupted by the withdrawal of Cameroon just before it kicked off. In June this year Namibia restated their claim for a place under the RWC sun, by winning the second CAR division ahead of Botswana, Tunisia and hosts Senegal at the Iba Mar Diop Stadium in Dakar. This should enable them to join Kenya, Madagascar and Zimbabwe in the third round of the African qualifiers next year, with the winners going to Pool C of RWC 2015 alongside New Zealand, Argentina, Tonga, and Europe 1, and the runners-up to the first round of the Repechage.

The perennial question before the start of every Asian qualifying zone has always been 'Who will be the runners-up to Japan?' rather than who will qualify for the next RWC, such is the abyss between the leading Asian power and the rest of the field. The qualifying zone commenced with a quadrangular tournament involving Sri Lanka, Chinese Taipei, Singapore and the hosts Philippines, in which the local team surprised the world and themselves by winning it undefeated. Further up the qualifying tree, a disappointing People's Republic of China got annihilated 89-0 by Malaysia and soundly beaten 52-3 by the newly emerged Iran. However, some 13 months and 31 matches later the predicted outcome materialised, with Japan breezing through to qualify for England 2015, scoring 316 points to eight against in their four matches, including a 121-0 destruction of the up-and-coming Philippines. Korea defeated Hong Kong 43-22 to secure the runners-up position and with it the right to play in the Repechage against the losers of the Americas final play-off.

With four unions – New Zealand, Australia, Samoa and Tonga – of the 12-strong Oceania (FORU) Zone already qualified, the brief RWC qualifying process involved in the first round only four of the remaining eight unions: Solomon Islands, Tahiti, Papua New Guinea and Cook Islands. The fifth, Fiji, take on the winners of the Oceania Cup tournament held in Port Moresby in Papua New Guinea in a home and away play-off for the Oceania 1 qualifying slot in Pool A of RWC 2015. For reasons unknown, the other five – Niue, Tuvalu, American Samoa, Wallis and Futuna, and New Caledonia – did not enter. It was clear from the outset that hosts Papua New Guinea and Cook Islands were the strongest, though Solomon Islands proved tough opponents. Indeed, their 23-22 bronze medal win over a surprisingly resourceful Tahiti (thanks to a late try by their burly loose-head prop Fredson Pukefenua and more significantly its 80th-minute conversion by outside half Leslie Puia) was well deserved. In the winner-takes-all final, the hosts started strongly and scored two tries through their scrum half Dougie Guise and left wing Henry Liliket to lead 12-3 after some 30 minutes of play. But the Cook islanders did not panic and came back strongly with a try by loose-head prop Jacob Marsters followed by a brace of tries, on either side of the break, by their speedy left wing Ioane Ioane. They never relinquished the lead and two more tries by outside half Greg Mullany and wing forward Francis Smith put the match beyond the efforts of the locals. The 37-31 win offers Cook Islands a shot at RWC immortality. However, it looks highly unlikely that they will be able to handle the Fijian firepower and unfortunately the outcome of the zone, very much like Japan in Asia, is very much a foregone conclusion. The only question is not will Fiji qualify, but by how many points.

With all the Six Nations already qualified, 69 matches will have been played by the end of the year in the qualifying rounds of the European Zone – 15 for Europe 1 and 2, the two starting positions in Pools C and D, and 54 for the right to challenge the third-placed European Nations Cup team for a place in the Repechage.

The coaches of the main three contenders – Georgia, Romania and Russia – must be reasonably happy with their progress so far, though Russia's Kingsley Jones felt hard done by at the size of his side's 29-14 defeat at the hands of Romania. For both Georgia's Milton Haig and Romania's Lynn Howells, it was business as usual, as their sides share the top position in the ENC table with four wins and a draw each. The appointment of the experienced Howells after the disastrous November series has been a blessing for Romania. Howells having been around for several months as FRR director of rugby, the new appointment did not come as a complete change of scenery for him. There was, however, a rather subtle reordering of priorities, making the RWC 2015 qualifying matches in the European Nations Cup the main objective. The best available players got selected for ENC matches and Romania played to win, which they did in increasingly confident fashion.

There is no easy match in the top division of the ENC nowadays and both Romania and Georgia should expect a strong Russian backlash in the away matches next year. A successful Russian campaign in 2014 may well change the qualifying scenario, with the bottom three also-rans – Portugal, Spain and Belgium – also able to upset the apple cart. The Portuguese had a patchy season, which cost their capable coach Errol Brain his job, and will be keen to show what they are made of. Spain, who decided to drop their comparatively successful French coach Régis Sonnes for New Zealander Bryce Bevin, in his second stint as national coach, performed below expectations, but although they seem out of contention for England 2015, they should not be taken lightly. Belgium have shown that they are not out of their depth at this level, but they are not yet ready for RWC action. The ENC table before the resumption of the competition, with Georgia and Romania sharing the top position and Russia third, is a good indication of the likely outcome of the zone, but it is too early to predict with any degree of certainty which one will be heading into the Repechage.

**BELOW** Romania full back Catalin Fercu on the burst against Russia in Bucharest.

# Plug into
# our network

**Harry Hyman of...**

# NEXUS

**and**

**Investor**Publishing

## Pleased to support
## Wooden Spoon

The UK Rugby
children's charity

As specialist healthcare and education industry
advisers and investors we provide a range of business
and management services, including:

- Corporate finance advice
- Private equity services
- Property fund management
- Real estate advisory services.

Publishers of:
HealthInvestor
EducationInvestor

www.healthinvestor.co.uk
www.educationinvestor.co.uk

# Staging the Cup
## the Venues for RWC 2015

### by CHRIS JONES

'Seven of the 13 tournament stadia are club football grounds, but only two are homes to Premiership rugby union teams – Exeter's Sandy Park and Kingsholm at Gloucester'

The surprise was that anyone was surprised when the final list of venues for the 2015 Rugby World Cup in England was revealed. The cup is the main source of income for the International Rugby Board and a nice earner for the host country – and size is everything when you are aiming to sell 2.5 million tickets.

Eden Park in Auckland staged the 2011 final between present champions New Zealand and France, but less than 60,000 fans were in a ground that ticks all the boxes when it comes to history and atmosphere but just doesn't have enough seats to generate the required income for the tournament. The New Zealand government covered the shortfall to ensure the tournament did not make a loss, which meant that the next hosts had to sign up for a guarantee to the IRB of a staggering £80 million.

It is after that bundle of dosh is handed over that England – and Wales, who host some of the key matches – can hope to cash in on actually having one of the planet's biggest sporting events on their land. To satisfy that guarantee, organisers had no option but to go for the big-capacity venues with plenty of corporate boxes, such as Wembley, the Olympic Stadium, Twickenham and the Millennium Stadium, and back

*BELOW* Twickenham, May 2013. Debbie Jevans, chief executive of England Rugby 2015, is flanked by RWC Limited chairman Bernard Lapasset (right) and RWCL managing director Brett Gosper at the announcement of the RWC 2015 schedule.

### RWC 2015 Venues

| Venue | Capacity | Location |
|---|---|---|
| Twickenham | 81,605 | London |
| Wembley | 90,256 | London |
| Olympic Stadium | 54,000 | London |
| Millennium Stadium | 74,154 | Cardiff |
| Etihad Stadium | 47,800 | Manchester |
| St James' Park | 52,409 | Newcastle |
| Elland Road | 37,914 | Leeds |
| King Power Stadium | 32,312 | Leicester |
| Villa Park | 42,785 | Birmingham |
| Kingsholm | 16,115 | Gloucester |
| Stadium MK | 30,717 | Milton Keynes |
| Amex Stadium | 30,750 | Brighton |
| Sandy Park | 12,300 | Exeter |

them up with some of England's most famous football stadia.

Seven of the 13 tournament stadia are club football grounds, but only two are homes to Premiership rugby union teams – Exeter's Sandy Park and Kingsholm at Gloucester. That meant great rugby arenas such as Welford Road in Leicester and Northampton's small but perfectly formed Franklin's Gardens could not host matches, even though a sell-out would be easy to achieve. What ruled them out of the equation was a failure to meet the 'footprint' test. While the playing area may have been big enough, neither ground satisfied the footprint, which involves run-off areas, perimeter boarding positions and the like that also form such a big part of the commercial income.

It is the nature of international sport that money rules and while the tournament will suffer from not embracing tried-and-tested venues, the organisers are bullish about their chances of making it a major financial and sporting triumph. Their own ranks have seen considerable change just a couple of years out from the event, with the chief executive role at the 2015 Rugby World Cup now held by Debbie Jevans, who was director of sport for the London 2012 Olympics.

Patently, here is a woman who knows how to run a major sporting event and manage the myriad different aspects that need to come together to make it a thumping success. It is a challenge that

Jevans is relishing as she told MihirBose.com, stating: 'Friends said it's got to be easier than the Olympics. You had 26 sports to organise [for 2012] versus one sport now.

'Actually it isn't. The scale of the Olympics is absolutely unique. This is on a smaller scale but it is still the third biggest sports event after the Olympics and the World Cup. And the complexity is still the same: the road closures, the transport system, the venues, teams, hotels. I may only have a staff of 300 compared to 1,000 in 2012 but, in attention to detail and difficulty, 2015 will be the same as 2012.

'We have a lot of tickets to sell. The IRB demand certain facilities, lay down very strict criteria and football clubs are currently those that offer them. Hence, we've used some of them. But, as at the Olympics where we had athletes at heart, we've got rugby teams at heart, so that was the main reason for this choice.'

Twelve teams have qualified for the finals – Australia, England and Wales in Pool A; South Africa, Samoa and Scotland in Pool B; New Zealand, Argentina and Tonga in Pool C; and France, Ireland and Italy in Pool D.

Each pool will be made up of five teams, with eight places to be filled via a series of qualifying matches which will be concluded in 2014 – and then the world of rugby will turn up in London for the second time in the history of the tournament.

In 1991, England lost to Australia in the final, but that tournament was spread all over the place because every country wanted a piece of the action. This time it is only Wales who are joining the party and that's due to the marvellous Millennium Stadium. Of course, Welsh support when it came to voting for the 2015 hosts was also very useful!

The World Cup is being designed along the same lines as the Olympics in terms of legacy – the word that was nailed onto the 2012 Games. Rugby did not make the most of 1991 in England, when playing numbers increased but this boost was not recognised properly or utilized by rugby chiefs. Jevans insists that this time all the youngsters attracted to the game will be given the chance to love the sport and make it their winter choice of activity.

'It will be a success if we've been inclusive and the players and the fans say, "That was amazing. I had a great time,"' she added. 'If the fans say the "fan zones were great. The journey was great. The sport was great" we will be successful. We need to make sure we have some unforgettable memories and celebrate the unique values of rugby.

'Just as 2012 was the catalyst to inspire a generation, 2015 is also the catalyst from which we want to bring more people into the game, to encourage more people to participate. I want to embrace the nation.

'If you think of 1966, you think football. If you think 2012 you think Olympic and Paralympic Games. I'd like to think that, when people think 2015, they will instantly think rugby. Rugby is a sport I'm passionate about and the opportunity to deliver the World Cup in a country I'm passionate about was something I just couldn't turn down. To deliver the Rugby World Cup is a challenge. But I'm really up for it.'

*LEFT* Gloucester's stronghold of Kingsholm is one of only two Premiership rugby stadia to make the list of RWC 2015 venues. Seven of the venues are club football grounds.

# Summer Tours 2013
## England in Argentina

### by HUGH GODWIN

'Down time was used variously for visiting the tomb of Eva Perón or posing for souvenir photos in La Boca with a Diego Maradona lookalike'

There were echoes in this three-match England tour to South America of a similar fixture schedule in summer 1997, when the then head coach Jack Rowell had an almighty row with the Lions, who were in South Africa and ordered him to release his fly half Mike Catt between the first and second Tests with the Pumas. The difference this year, when Christian Wade and Billy Twelvetrees received a summons from the Lions in Australia after sharing in England's win over Argentina in the first Test, was that their head coach Stuart Lancaster waved them off with a cheery smile – publicly, at least.

The reasons for Lancaster's even-tempered restraint were not all to do with savvier public relations. In 1997 Rowell's tenure with England was coming to an end and he was concerned only with completing what would have been a first clean sweep by a Home Union on a two-Test tour of Argentina (much as he'd feared, without Catt, England were well beaten in the second Test).

Lancaster knew the Pumas of 2013 were a much less formidable bunch due to the phenomenon of modern fixture-making that obliges their Europe-based stars to miss the June incoming tour in favour of the higher-profile Rugby Championship from August to October. Moreover, Lancaster's focus was firmly on development for the 2015 World Cup. The opportunity to cap Gloucester's Jonny May as Wade's stand-in on the wing was far from detrimental to the aims of the trip.

Sure enough, Lancaster's England added victory by 51-26 in the second Test at Vélez Sarsfield in Buenos Aires to their initial salvo, a 32-3 thumping of the Pumas in Salta. It was England's first clean sweep in Argentina, and their second series win after Bill Beaumont's team won one Test and drew one in 1981. In Home Union terms, it emulated the 2-0 successes by Wales in 1999 and Scotland in 2010.

The tour began, in terms of a squad getting together, with the 40-12 win over a terribly lacklustre Barbarians at Twickenham on 26 May, but it had a more authentic feel in Montevideo on the first Sunday in June when a non-cap England met a team representing Consur (the South American Rugby Confederation). Old Christians, the club sadly famous for their Andes aeroplane crash in the 1970s, scored a last-minute try to win the curtain-raiser against Carrasco Polo accompanied by fervent crowd noise and firecrackers; England, by contrast, were greeted with respectful applause as they ran out, on their first visit to Uruguay. The Wasps No. 8 Billy Vunipola, who will play for Saracens alongside his brother Mako next season, rumbled and bundled his way to three tries in a slightly stuttering 41-21 win.

The first Lions call came the following Wednesday, when England's loose-head prop Alex Corbisiero left for Australia, with Lancaster cancelling an Andean cable-car jaunt to deal with the fallout. He chose five new caps for the first Test: Wade and flanker Matt Kvesic from the start, and Vunipola, Bath centre Kyle Eastmond and Sale tight-head prop Henry Thomas as second-half substitutes. Rarely has such a new-look team won a Tier One international away from home so emphatically. Three tries had England 25-3 ahead at half-time, and while the Pumas had plugged one gap by recalling the 35-year-old Felipe Contepomi at inside centre for his eightieth cap, their once-proud scrummage was sadly supine. Opposite Contepomi it was

*FACING PAGE* Veteran Argentine centre Felipe Contepomi, winning his eightieth cap, stands in the way of a charging Billy Vunipola during the first Test in Salta.

*BELOW* Marland Yarde, who scored two tries in the game, makes a break during the second Test in Buenos Aires.

fascinating to witness the Gloucester midfield duo of Freddie Burns, 23, and Twelvetrees, 24, because they reflected a footballing style professed as a preference by Lancaster in his early days as England coach but hitherto rarely seen on the field.

Wade, the Wasps flyer who had enjoyed a terrific domestic season, had his head trodden on after he chased the first kick-off, but he quickly recovered as England defended a series of 12 Argentina phases with hard, low tackling and dominated the scrum to earn the positions for Burns to kick two penalty goals before the tries scored by Saracens wing David Strettle, Twelvetrees and Gloucester No. 8 Ben Morgan after 17, 25 and 31 minutes respectively. Wade combined with Morgan and Kvesic through the middle to set up the first, and Kvesic linked several times for the second; Wade gave the final pass for the second and third. Soft Argentina tackling played its part and, interestingly, considering the critical comment to come on the Lions tour, the initial breakout had begun when New Zealander referee Chris Pollock allowed Bath hooker Rob Webber – on his feet – to make a turnover after the tackle.

When Burns kicked out on the full early in the second half, England's tight five of Joe Marler, Webber, David Wilson, Joe Launchbury and Dave Attwood had a scrum to defend on their 22. No problem. The Pumas were firmly held, and although their backs breached the gain line for a change, England's forwards covered around athletically, and Twelvetrees, meeting tackles in his pleasingly square-on fashion, helped clear the danger. Argentina's full back Martín Bustos Moyano missed three penalties, England scrummaged and counter-rucked hard in their own 22 to deal with another threat in the 65th minute, and eventually Vunipola scored their fourth try from another powerful if messy scrum, just after the 80-minute hooter had gone (and no matter that Pollock, oddly, whistled before the 20-year-old Wasp had even grounded the ball).

Twelvetrees departed in the following midweek, while Wade received the call on the Saturday of the second Test, together with Brad Barritt who was holidaying in the United States as one of five England regulars – the others were Chris Ashton, Danny Care, Toby Flood and Chris Robshaw – who had been rested from the trip but reportedly assured by Lancaster of their place in the following season's senior squad. The familiar face of Catt was back in Buenos Aires now as Lancaster's attacking skills coach, alongside the tour's temporary staff: Rob Baxter and Paul Gustard, covering for the Lions forwards coach Graham Rowntree and defence coach Andy Farrell respectively. Down time was used variously for visiting the tomb of Eva Perón or posing for souvenir photos in La Boca with a Diego Maradona lookalike. And so to a lively atmosphere at Vélez Sarsfield, where the Pumas made a change in each row of the scrum, moved Contepomi in to fly half and adopted tighter, pick-and-go tactics, while England fielded their youngest back division since the loss to Wales at Wembley in 1999.

Penalties by Bustos Moyano and Burns (who had Eastmond and his soon to be Bath clubmate Jonathan Joseph as his centres) contributed to a 12-6 lead for Argentina after 26 minutes, reflecting their greater share of possession and territory, before a quick line out taken by England full back Mike Brown to himself earned good field position and a put-in by Lee Dickson to a scrum. Burns grubber-kicked towards the posts, Bustos Moyano carried over his line, and referee Nigel Owens did not hesitate to award England's unchanged pack a penalty try as Argentina buckled away from the resulting scrum. England had a second try on 37 minutes when Burns finished a sequence of 11

*RIGHT* Open-side flanker Matt Kvesic, on his way to Gloucester for the new season, gets stuck in as England beat the Pumas 51-26 in the Argentine capital. Kvesic was among the players who took 'definitive steps forward' on the tour.

phases. Demoralisingly for Argentina, there was time for a second penalty try at the scrum and England led 25-12 at half-time.

Wing Manuel Montero finally gave Argentina their first try of the series, with 49 minutes gone, but England pulled clear, with Webber scoring in the 55th minute, to be followed over twice by May's fellow wing debutant Marland Yarde of London Irish. The first try was from a bullocking short-side burst that exposed Argentina's defence after a line out; the second was illuminated by an expert inside pass from Eastmond, the convert from rugby league, who contributed a skipping, jinking score of his own in between. Northampton fly half Stephen Myler had a first cap from the bench.

It left Contepomi to comment admiringly that Lancaster would be spoilt for choice in his next selection. 'The way I sell it,' Lancaster explained, 'is that it [the Elite and Saxons squads combined] is a 66-man squad and if someone is playing well enough we will find a way to get them into the senior squad and give them an opportunity. It makes it challenging.'

Among those to take definitive steps forward were Kvesic, the Worcester open-side newly signed by Gloucester, whose breakaway running and incessant link play unlocked the door to a wider-ranging style. Bath lock Attwood was relieved to discover there was life in his England career after injury and disciplinary problems, while Launchbury, Morgan and Tom Wood – who assumed the captaincy with easy authority on and off the field – were established players reasserting their rights. By contrast, David Strettle and Courtney Lawes could have had happier trips. As for Saracens' Alex Goode and Joel Tomkins, who missed out injured, and Northampton's Dylan Hartley, the suspended hooker who would have been with the Lions, they were among those left to wonder how much the pecking order might have altered.

# SARACENS SPORT FOUNDATION

"Inspiring communities and changing lives through the power of sport"

**www.saracens.com/foundation**

Allianz Park, Greenlands Lane, Barnet, London, NW4 1RL
Tel: 0203 675 7245 Registered charity no: 1079316

# Scotland in South Africa

## by ALAN LORIMER

'But in a last-gasp effort Alasdair Strokosch exploited a mistake by Sergio Parisse in the defensive line to stroll over for a try, Laidlaw's conversion producing victory at the death'

It may not have generated the hoped-for results, but Scotland's participation in the Castle Lager quadrangular series alongside Samoa, Italy and host nation South Africa may yet prove to have been an astute move.

The records tell a tale of played three, lost two, won one. But while the loss to Samoa deserved the negative comments that followed, the defeat to South Africa in Nelspruit showed what Scotland can achieve if they get their performance right. Victory over Italy proved that fortune can occasionally smile on Scotland.

This was a tour to test new players at international level. Scott Johnson, Scotland's interim coach, has made it clear he wants to broaden the base of potential international players and increase competition for places. The quadrangular tournament in South Africa was the perfect opportunity to do so. 'I don't want players turning up thinking they're an automatic selection and that goes for the Lions boys, too. I think that we're a bit further down that track but we're not finished,' said Johnson at the conclusion of the tour.

**ABOVE** Sean Lamont goes over in the corner for Scotland's try in the 27-17 defeat to Samoa in the Castle Incoming Series quadrangular tournament in South Africa. It was Samoa's first win over Scotland.

Johnson's tour party was without what was initially a trio of Lions players that then became a quartet when Ryan Grant received a call-up from Warren Gatland. Moreover, injuries and the need for recuperation necessitated that a good number of players, including fly half Duncan Weir, centre Nick De Luca and hookers Ross Ford and Dougie Hall spent the summer at home.

Of course in a Lions year this is a familiar scenario for any of the Home Unions and inevitably results in a bundle of new caps emerging. In the case of Scotland, which has only two professional teams and a small base of talented juniors, blooding new international players is an essential part of the tour process.

Over the three matches in the quadrangular tournament, ten Scotland players – six backs and four forwards – made their international debuts and certainly several of these will represent their country again in the future. Among the new caps who caught the eye were full back Peter Murchie, centre Alex Dunbar, centre/fly half Peter Horne, wing Tommy Seymour, centre/wing Duncan Taylor and lock Tim Swinson.

Sadly Horne suffered a serious knee injury against South Africa and will be sidelined for this season. That is a blow not only for the Glasgow player but also for Scotland's coaching team. Horne's injury was one of several setbacks for Scotland, skipper Kelly Brown, prop Geoff Cross and hooker Pat MacArthur being forced to return home after what was a brutal opening match against Samoa.

If the tour offered opportunities for newcomers, it also allowed some recent caps to enhance their reputations, notably centre Matt Scott, who at the end of his second season as an international player looked a much more mature performer and one who has solved what was an ongoing problem at inside centre.

Back-row David Denton, too, gave a timely reminder that he is an excellent ball carrier, while hooker Scott Lawson put together his best set of performances in a Scotland jersey, prop Jon Welsh made a strong case for national selection and Henry Pyrgos showed his dynamic game at scrum half makes him a perfect impact player.

Of the experienced caps in the tour party, Sean Lamont looked an invigorated player (perhaps because he received a few more passes than usual), Jim Hamilton, despite an indiscretion in the South Africa game, was bedrock material and on the flank Alasdair Strokosch led by example.

Then there was Greig Laidlaw, who is the most recent in a long line of international scrum halves from the Scottish Borders. Like his famous uncle, Roy, Greig proved to be an excellent and natural leader, the Edinburgh No. 9 having taken over the captaincy following the departure home of Kelly Brown.

Quietly spoken, Laidlaw has the respect of his team-mates, who appreciate his tactical nous on the field and his Borders down-to-earth approach away from the action. Add to that his accurate goal-kicking, not least the winning conversion goal against Italy, and it's easy to see why he and Johnson complement one another.

There was always the fear that coming into the tournament after a lengthy lay-off could be risky. In the event these fears proved not unfounded as Scotland faced Samoa in the first round of the tournament at the ABSA Stadium in Durban.

Samoa, ranked seventh in the world to Scotland's twelfth, had reason to feel confident, the more so having defeated Wales in Cardiff in 2012. Scotland went into the match having never lost to Samoa, but the ninth meeting between the two countries was to end that record.

Against a Scotland side off the pace, Samoa used their powerful players to make inroads into the Scots' defence, scoring two tries early on through James So'oialo and the juggernaut Alesana Tuilagi, answered by a try from Sean Lamont.

Scotland managed to work their way back into the game and levelled the scores at 17-17, only for Tuilagi to power over for a second try, and with the conversion kick successful and a penalty to follow, Samoa finished winners by 27-17.

In his post-match conference Johnson said: 'This was the first Test for a few and a lot of the others were inexperienced. I was in Australia when England sent out a so-called second-string side that spawned the World Cup-winning team. Careers start in funny ways.'

With South Africa to follow seven days later, there was a feeling of dread amongst Scotland fans and a feeling too within South Africa that

*FACING PAGE* Scotland lock Alastair Kellock tries to charge down Jeremy Su'a's clearance kick, against Samoa in Durban.

*BELOW* Alasdair Dickinson, the Scotland loose-head, is felled by the Samoa defence.

the Boks would win by a 40-point margin. Fifty minutes into the Test at Nelspruit, when Scotland led 17-6, many of the so-called pundits who had made that prediction would have handed over a few rand to find a hiding place.

The Scots had defied everyone, including themselves, it seemed. Playing with passion, accuracy, strength, tenacious tackling and with tactical awareness, the Scots took the game to South Africa and were rewarded with tries by Matt Scott and Alex Dunbar and goals from Greig Laidlaw.

Then the turning point. Scotland after giving away a penalty try then lost Jim Hamilton to the sin-bin. The big lock had pushed his opposite number Eben Etzebeth in the face after a period of prolonged niggling, but neither referee Romain Poite nor his assistant felt able to make a decision and called for the TMO to look at the incident closely. The verdict from above was that the offence merited a yellow card, and Scotland from being in a good position to win were fatally weakened.

South Africa seized their opportunity, with a converted try for JJ Engelbrecht putting them ahead for the first time in the game. And with a bench of proven Test players and top Super Rugby performers to bring on, it was advantage South Africa. A penalty by Pat Lambie and his conversion of a late try by Jan Serfontein then gave the Boks a flattering scoreline and victory.

Scotland had raised their game massively but finished with a disappointing defeat and in the process suffered tour-ending injuries to fly half Ruaridh Jackson and his replacement Peter Horne.

Loftus Versfeld in Pretoria was the venue for the third and final match against Italy. But after the Herculean effort against South Africa, Scotland's performance against the Italians was flat. Italy know they can always subdue the Scots with powerful scrummaging and this latest encounter was no different.

**BELOW** Henry Pyrgos and the Scotland team rush to congratulate Alasdair Strokosch, whose last-ditch try has made a Scottish victory possible against Italy in Pretoria.

It seemed Italy's forward-orientated game and their ability to slow down the ball had earned the Azzurri victory when they led 29-23 with full-time showing on the stadium clock. But in a last-gasp effort Alasdair Strokosch exploited a mistake by Sergio Parisse in the defensive line to stroll over for a try, Laidlaw's conversion producing victory at the death.

'Lucky, yes,' said Johnson, adding: 'Never doubt our perseverance. We will dog it out to the end.' Words that will be repeated, no doubt.

# Wales in Japan

## by GRAHAM CLUTTON

'If nothing else, the summer tour to Japan has proved that the conveyor belt of talent that has fed the Wales national side so well in recent times is still as productive as it ever has been'

Selection for the first tour to Japan since the summer of 2001 wasn't exactly a case of 'last men standing', but for coach Robin McBryde, the task of assembling a party good enough to beat one of the world's emerging nations was to say the least intriguing.

With 15 players on British & Irish Lions duty, several others unavailable due to injury and a handful of senior players deliberately overlooked, McBryde named a squad with nine uncapped players. Instead of Ryan Jones, Paul James and James Hook, McBryde opted for the likes of Rhys Patchell, Dan Baker and Scott Baldwin, amongst many other rookies.

Sadly, after winning the first Test in Osaka, 22-18, Wales underperformed in Tokyo as the Cherry Blossoms, for the first time in their modest rugby history, beat Wales to level the series. A disappointing way to end the tour, for McBryde, in terms of the result, but when Gatland returned from Australia for the debrief, results were the last item on the agenda.

'I made the decisions and I backed this group of young men,' McBryde said. 'Yes, we've fallen short, but hopefully the experience these young men will have gained will put them in good stead.

'I'm not going to hang my head in shame because it's important that we learn from this and move on. Obviously we're disappointed to have lost the second Test. We paid the ultimate price for not only being inaccurate, but failing to make the most of our opportunities. Had we have taken those opportunities we would have been in a strong position at half-time.

*BELOW* Wales back-row Dan Baker, in his second international, is wrapped up by Japan's Justin Ives in the second Test in Tokyo, which was won by the hosts to give them their first win over a major rugby country.

'But you can't take anything away from Japan, they showed what a quality side they are and if you allow them to play with that tempo in their game, they're going to be a match for any team.

'They're very competitive against Samoa, Fiji and Tonga [in the Pacific Nations Cup], so they're an experienced bunch of men. They fully deserved their victory but we could have done our work better.'

Despite suffering the ignominy of being the man in charge when Wales suffered their first defeat by Japan, McBryde believed the members of his inexperienced squad would learn some valuable lessons from the tour.

'They've been thrown together at the end of a tough season, different backgrounds the majority of them. You don't know how far to push yourself until you push yourself that little bit too far, maybe that was the case.'

McBryde named four new caps in his side for the first Test and though the side came under heavy pressure at times, they hung on to register a satisfactory victory. They lacked a genuine open-side on the day, although Ospreys blind-side James King stood out as one of the players to commend. Teenage wing Dafydd Howells stuck to his task, while Jonathan Spratt, playing his first Test since 2009, was certainly not out of place.

Bradley Davies captained the side and paid tribute to the deep-seated determination of his players in temperatures that soared into the high thirties Celsius (hundreds Fahrenheit). 'It was difficult, very hot and humid, but I felt the guys stuck to their task well. It was a very young side, but we showed some signs of ambition and I'm satisfied with how we stood up to the task.'

Harry Robinson's second-half score proved to be the key moment, the Cardiff Blues wing scoring Wales's only try following a wonderful assist from impressive full back Liam Williams. The Scarlets youngster has already proved himself on the international stage and will relish the opportunity to shadow Leigh Halfpenny in the upcoming autumn international series.

Japan actually outscored Wales two tries to one in that first Test, Michael Broadhurst and Yoshikazu Fujita their scorers either side of the interval. Broadhurst's score and the boot of Ayumu

Goromaru had given the Blossoms an 11-6 half-time lead, but a couple of missed penalties came back to haunt them.

In contrast, it was the boot of Dan Biggar that kept Wales in the game, though they did struggle at times against the physicality of their hosts and endured an even tougher ten minutes at one stage when Scarlets back-rower Rob McCusker received a yellow card.

If the satisfaction of winning the first Test was unbounded, the disappointment of losing the second was frustrating to an equivalent degree. Second-half tries from Craig Wing and Broadhurst proved decisive for Japan as Wales paid the price for their inaccuracy in the final third.

Tom Prydie was Wales's try scorer, while Biggar added a penalty. However, it was the home side who managed the game better, especially in the second half, to secure victory.

When the dust settled on the series, the disappointment of losing the second Test was more than offset by the satisfaction of seeing such a young, inexperienced squad represent Wales in the absence of so many of Gatland's senior stars.

Andries Pretorius was one of the players to make his debut and to show McBryde enough in terms of quality and understanding to suggest that in the wake of the Lions tour, he will get a second chance. In a world of big hits, the South African-born forward boasts the necessary arsenal not only to cope with the rigours of international rugby but to prosper too.

Behind the scrum, Patchell is a young pivot whose next opportunity will come sooner rather than later. The Cardiff Blues outside half, who kicked a late penalty in the first Test at Osaka, could have played for Wales in the Under 20 World Championship, but was deemed suitable to become Biggar's understudy in the heat of Japan. With pace to burn and bucketfuls of confidence, Patchell provided glimpses of the talent that lies within.

Welsh rugby might have fallen behind in terms of its ability to compete in the Heineken Cup, but if nothing else, the summer tour to Japan has proved that the conveyor belt of talent that has fed the national side so well in recent times is still as productive as it ever has been.

**FACING PAGE** Right wing Harry Robinson touches down for Wales's solitary try in Osaka.

**BELOW** Tour skipper Bradley Davies on the rampage for Wales in the first Test.

# ANATOMY *of the* PROFIT.

## The hunter must get *under the skin* of his quarry.

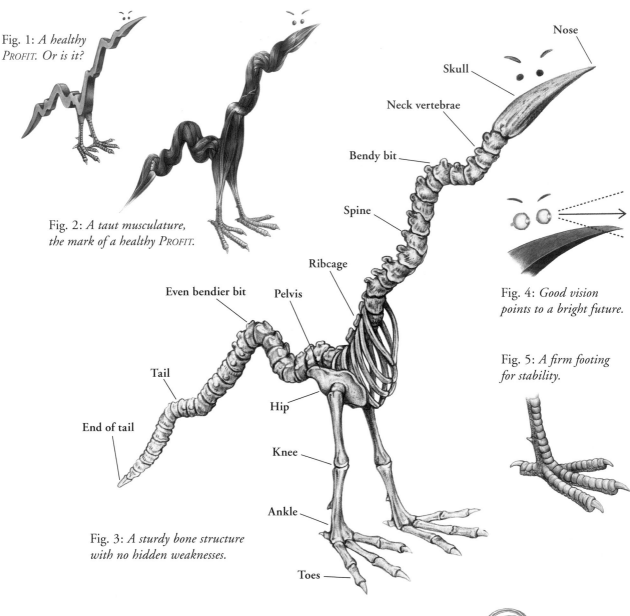

Fig. 1: *A healthy* PROFIT. *Or is it?*

Fig. 2: *A taut musculature, the mark of a healthy* PROFIT.

Nose

Skull

Neck vertebrae

Bendy bit

Spine

Ribcage

Even bendier bit

Pelvis

Tail

Hip

End of tail

Knee

Ankle

Toes

Fig. 4: *Good vision points to a bright future.*

Fig. 5: *A firm footing for stability.*

Fig. 3: *A sturdy bone structure with no hidden weaknesses.*

If you'd like to get under the skin of Profits and Profit Hunting, speak to your financial adviser. Alternatively contact us on the details below. Please remember that past performance should not be seen as a guide to future performance. The value of any investment and any income from it can fall as well as rise as a result of market and currency fluctuations and you may not get back the amount originally invested.

## ARTEMIS
### The PROFIT Hunter

**0800 092 2051**    **investorsupport@artemisfunds.com**    **artemis.co.uk**

Issued by Artemis Fund Managers Limited which is authorised and regulated by the Financial Conduct Authority (www.fca.org.uk), 25 The North Colonnad Canary Wharf, London E14 5HS. For your protection calls are usually recorded.

# Ireland in North America

## by RUAIDHRI O'CONNOR

'The New Zealander saw less-heralded players step up and be counted as the States sensed a first win over Ireland – a first indeed over a top-tier nation – was on the cards'

Ireland's players watched the ball sail over the bar, mopped their sodden brows and contemplated being on the wrong side of history. They were an unfamiliar team, in a strange place, in uncomfortably hot conditions and, with 15 minutes to go, they led the US Eagles by just three points and the momentum was with the Americans.

When they looked around they saw a collection of new caps, first starters and a handful of regular extended-squad members. With Mike Ross and Simon Zebo off, just one of them would have been considered first choice when the full squad was available. That was the captain, Peter O'Mahony, and he led the recovery on a hot night in Houston in front of a record crowd of 21,081 at the BBVA Compass Stadium.

Watching from the stand was Joe Schmidt, the man appointed to lead Ireland out of the perennial slump that had engulfed them in the Declan Kidney era. He wasn't in charge, but it was the first game of his era and defeat would not have been a good start. That Ireland got through it and then went on to beat Canada comfortably a week later meant that the tour could be filed away as a success. It almost wasn't the start he wanted.

The New Zealander saw less-heralded players step up and be counted as the States sensed a first win over Ireland – a first indeed over a top-tier nation – was on the cards at only 15-12 down.

> **BELOW** Andrew Trimble, making his fiftieth Test appearance for Ireland, scores his country's first try of the match against Canada in Toronto.

They threw everything into it, but Ireland responded. O'Mahony tackled like a demon, Paul Marshall found space with a darting run and Devin Toner made two plays befitting of his stature as the game's biggest man.

Perhaps the most significant moment came, however, when a loose kick reached Biarritz's Taku Ngwenya, one of the most dangerous runners in rugby. The winger took off, and all that stood between him and acres of space was replacement winger Felix Jones. The Munsterman made his tackle, debutant Stuart Olding got in over the ball and forced the penalty that, although missed by Ian Madigan, earned enough time to get Ireland over the line.

It was not a victory to live long in the memory, but defeat would have hung like a dark cloud over the players' and interim coach Les Kiss's heads for some time.

Just ask out-half Madigan, who heaped pressure on himself, the coach and the captain on the eve of the game. 'If we put ourselves in the boots of the US Eagles, they're going to see this as an opportunity because we're missing ten of our best players and because it's an away game,' he said.

'If they want to have any aspirations of doing well at the next World Cup then they have to beat us, they have to be able to beat teams like us on their home patch because if they don't the fact of the matter is they'll just be making up the numbers. They'd say that themselves.

'For that reason there's a different type of pressure on this game, there's reputations on the line. If we lose the three main people who will take the brunt of it are myself, Peter O'Mahony and Les.

'I'd be more nervous on that side of things than against Australia or France where if you're slightly off your game you could lose by 30 or 40 points whereas if we're off our game here we could lose our reputations.'

Madigan was one of the young guns who delivered, kicking five out of six and looking assured in his first international start and his first appearance for Ireland at out-half.

Along with the 24-year-old, Ulster's Iain Henderson and Munster's Dave Kilcoyne finally began a game for their country, having been used off the bench for much of the season, while Olding and Connacht teenager Robbie Henshaw won their first caps. Both showed signs of huge promise, with Olding in particular looking at home as an international inside centre.

That duo were joined off the bench by fellow first caps in Munster's Tommy O'Donnell and Mike Sherry and Leinster's Jamie Hagan as the player base was expanded ahead of Schmidt's tenure officially beginning on 1 July.

Henshaw is one of Ireland's most exciting prospects, but the Connacht youngster had a nervy second half and missed an opportunity to mark his debut with a try, letting Fergus McFadden's pass slip through his hands. That would have made the score 17-6 with the conversion to come and there would have been no way back for the Americans.

Ireland were struggling in humid conditions, with the US back row of Samu Manoa, Scott LaValla and Todd Clever dominating the back-row contest. Despite skipper Clever being sent to the sin-bin for dangerous play, the Eagles managed to claw back the lead and the game went down to the wire, with Chris Wyles kicking his side within three before Ireland held out.

Ireland having survived, the match was quickly forgotten when Zebo received a call-up to the Lions via team manager Mick Kearney as soon as he arrived back at the team hotel. The winger's own phone had been ruined when he jumped into an ice-bath with it in his pocket.

*FACING PAGE* Ian Madigan, in his first Test start, slots one of his five penalties against the USA.

*BELOW* Leading by example. Ireland skipper Peter O'Mahony takes the game to the Eagles.

# LOCH FYNE®
### SEAFOOD & GRILL

———

*"We started life as a small shack selling oysters on Scotland's West Highland route at the head of Loch Fyne. Our fish is sustainably sourced, either from abundant wild stocks or responsibly farmed"*

———

- 42 restaurants nationwide, most of which are in unique historic or listed buildings

- A la carte menu with a wide range of fresh seafood and fish including our famous oysters and platters plus meat and vegetarian options

- Set menu available during daytime with 2 courses for £9.95

- Range of quality wines by the glass or bottle, selected by our Master wine buyer to complement our dishes

- Fresh fish and seafood available from our cold counter for you to purchase to cook at home

to find your local restaurant, view our menus or book a table, visit
### www.lochfyne-restaurants.com

It meant that the news cycle had moved swiftly on as he headed to Australia and the team travelled to Toronto, where the second Test, against Canada, awaited. Despite 11 members of the squad coming down with a stomach bug in the build-up to the game, Ireland had a far more comfortable night at the BMO Field in front of another record crowd of 20,396.

Kiss handed Munster journeyman James Downey his debut at 32, while experienced campaigners Kevin McLaughlin and Andrew Trimble were called into the team, with the Ulster player winning his fiftieth cap. He celebrated it with the opening try on what would be a night to remember for McFadden, who scored the first hat-trick by an Irish player in a Test since Kevin Maggs against Fiji in 2002. In all, Ireland ran in six tries, with Tommy O'Donnell marking an excellent first start with a good score and Darren Cave running in another as Ireland beat the Canadians comfortably, 40-14.

Again, O'Mahony had stepped up to the plate in an assured display that saw him police the opposition whenever he felt referee Leighton Hodges let them away with something. On a developmental tour, it was a coming of age for the 23-year-old Corkman, who looks like a captain in the making for the future.

At the end of what Kiss admitted had been a 'tough' year, there were reasons for Schmidt to be optimistic ahead of the beginning of his reign. 'All we could deal with was the here and now,' Kiss said. 'These guys had a mission they knew the purpose, look, we made it clear to them they really had to stand up, that if they wanted to be part of the future, if we needed to make a statement about Irish rugby finish this off, in all honesty this was the only time we had and they did do that and it was fantastic.'

With six new caps blooded and a number of players showing real promise as leaders, the squad headed off on their holidays satisfied with a job well done in North America.

How many of them will be involved when Samoa, Australia and New Zealand come to Dublin in November remains to be seen, but many did their cause no harm at all.

**BELOW** Against Canada, Fergus McFadden became the first player to score a Test hat-trick for Ireland since Kevin Maggs against Fiji in 2002.

NORTON ROSE FULBRIGHT

Wherever you are,
you're never that far
from **our support.**

As a global practice with close to 3800 lawyers in more than 50 offices around the world, people are our most important asset. So we're delighted to support Wooden Spoon and the efforts of all the people involved with this charity.

**Law around the world**
nortonrosefulbright.com

Financial institutions | Energy | Infrastructure, mining and commodities
Transport | Technology and innovation | Life sciences and healthcare

# HOME FRONT

# Pride of Worcester
## their Premiership 2012-13
### by SARA ORCHARD

'At the final whistle everybody was on the pitch – not just the players but supporters, coaches, friends and family. Everyone was crying and hugging each other'

For years we've turned to Worcestershire Sauce to give our cheese on toast that added spice – but few thought that 2013 would see a different export from the county provide a new surprise topping in English women's rugby.

Established in 1990, the Women's Rugby Premiership had become a bit of a London love-in. Richmond Ladies were the reigning champions and continue to have one of the biggest women's sections in England: they operate three teams and have produced over a hundred international players. Coached at present by former Scotland international and current Metropolitan Police Chief Inspector Karen Findlay, Richmond Ladies lifted the Women's Premiership title in 2010, 2011 and 2012. In the 2012-13 season Richmond hoped to become only the second side to win the Premiership for four consecutive seasons.

*FACING PAGE* Flanker Pippa Crews scores the try that ensures a bonus point against Wasps at Twyford Avenue, bringing the Premiership title to Worcester Ladies for the first time.

*RIGHT* Jenny Brightmore rises in the line out to claim the ball for Worcester against Darlington Mowden Park Sharks. Worcester did the double over the Sharks, winning 72-12 at home and 31-11 on the road.

Who could challenge Richmond Ladies as the new season approached? Saracens Ladies came closest the previous year, finishing second, and were the last club to lift the Premiership title before Richmond's three-in-a-row. The biggest threat outside the M25 was thought to be from Staffordshire. Home of the England Women's captain and No. 8 Sarah Hunter, Lichfield Ladies had great promise after finishing in third place for the last two seasons. As the search for a new challenger drew eyes down the list of the eight teams making up the 2012-13 Women's Premiership, few backed Worcester Ladies to be in the mix for the top spot.

Worcester No. 8 and co-captain Karen Jones: 'Worcester has always been a mid-table team. After finishing fifth the season before [2011-12] we were disappointed. It was really one of our coaches, Donna Kennedy, who turned round and said we needed to have self-belief and questioned: Why couldn't Worcester Ladies be Premiership winners?'

Worcester opened their 2012-13 account with an away victory over local rivals Lichfield on Sunday 9 September 2012. The 34-22 win in the Midlands derby gave off the first warning signal to the rest of the Premiership that Worcester Ladies were contenders. Karen Jones: 'We turned up on that day with a squad that hadn't had much time together due to international commitments, but we played some fantastic rugby and showed what we were capable of. It was the way we responded to being under pressure that excited us the most. Previously Worcester would have lost a game like that but from somewhere the self-belief and the ability to stand up under pressure kicked in. Had we not won that game I don't think the season would have panned out in the same way.'

The promising start continued for Worcester, who went ten games unbeaten, including a first win on the road against reigning champions Richmond. But the Worcester momentum was finally halted in April. In the space of eight days the title race was ripped wide open. Worcester lost twice – both times at home. Karen Jones: 'April was a very difficult month for us. We had players who'd been on international duty with the Six Nations who came back injured. Heather Fisher and Jo Watmore were out; Danielle Waterman came back but got injured early on. I had knee surgery so I was sidelined along with others – I think at that one time we had ten first-team players unavailable.'

On 7 April Worcester hosted Lichfield on the Sixways site at Weston's pitches. After the unbeaten run, many of the Worcester Wanderers men came along to support, including the club president, Michael Clarke. Most were stunned as Lichfield took their revenge for the opening-day loss, winning 37-7. Karen Jones: 'Dare I say it, some complacency had snuck in. People were starting to

think that "this is our league". It was a shock to the system. The league wasn't going to be given to us, we were going to have to fight for it.' The following Sunday Richmond Ladies arrived at Sixways. The reigning champions were still smarting from the result at Christmas and put themselves back in title contention with a 19-10 win.

Worcester averted disaster with a win against Saracens the following week, but their lead at the top of the table had narrowed to just one point going into the final weekend. The chasing team was Richmond Ladies. To guarantee lifting the title, Worcester needed a bonus-point win away at Wasps. Meanwhile, Richmond were playing just four miles away at the Athletic Ground, hosting Bristol. However, both clubs had depleted resources with many of their England internationals unavailable for selection.

Karen Jones: 'With none of the England Sevens players available it was tough. The RFU had told us at the start of the season that that would be the case. For the likes of Richmond and ourselves we had to go out and play the most important fixture of the season with half of our first-team squads missing. It wasn't just disappointing for the club it was disappointing for the players. The likes of Kat Merchant couldn't even be at the match where we secured the title. I know how hard that was for her – her heart is very much with Worcester.'

England wing Kat Merchant has played at Worcester for 13 years: 'After playing every game I was gutted not to be able to play in the final game, I had England Sevens training. I was 100 per cent behind the girls but it was an emotional day.' Merchant and other absent Worcester players had to rely on text and Twitter updates to know what was happening.

Worcester needed five tries to secure the bonus-point victory and become champions. The pre-match team talk at Twyford Avenue was memorable for Karen: 'I put in a huge amount of my own passion into my words as did my co-captain Jenny Mills. I've never seen Jenny be emotional before a game – but everyone knew how important it was to win. It was a very emotional and tense team talk and it obviously worked.'

The determination was clear. Outside centre Sarah Guest scored a brace and was joined on the scoresheet by Megan Goddard, Rochelle Clark, Charlotte Keane, Pippa Crews and Rhiannon

Watkins. The final score was 48-8, but more importantly the title was Worcester Ladies' for the first time.

Karen Jones: 'At the final whistle everybody was on the pitch – not just the players but supporters, coaches, friends and family. Everyone was crying and hugging each other. We've always been a club that plays for each other but it just meant so much to everyone – especially for those who've worked tirelessly for 21 years to build the club up. It was a very special moment.'

Kat Merchant: 'Even though I wasn't there, it's the highest achievement in club rugby and for many players the highlight of their rugby careers. Sarah Guest and myself have played at Worcester together for 13 years so to win the Premiership has been fantastic. I've been proud to play alongside Pippa Crews, Jen Mills and Sarah Guest to name a few. They are the girls who helped make the season so special.'

Karen Jones: 'It's good for women's rugby to have a different name on the Premiership Shield and we're under no illusions of how hard it's going to be. Lichfield are getting stronger, Richmond will want to bounce back, Wasps and Saracens are rebuilding and 2013-14 is going to be a really exciting season.

'Hopefully success breeds success and girls in the local area who previously might have moved away to play for one of the London clubs will now stay and play for Worcester. Looking forward we've just got to hope that this is just a stepping-stone to even greater things. We want Worcester Ladies to be a real force in women's rugby and not just a one-off season winner.'

There are already high hopes for the 2013-14 Women's Premiership season, with much at stake for the country's top players. England head coach Gary Street will be watching as he selects his squad to take to the 2014 World Cup in France next August.

*ABOVE* Worcester Ladies with the trophy after beating Wasps 48-8 to claim the Premiership for the first time. The victorious team that day comprised:
15 Zoe Bennion,
14 Sam Bree,
13 Sarah Guest,
12 Megan Goddard,
11 Charlotte Keane,
10 Ceri Large*,
9 Bianca Blackburn,
1 Rochelle Clark*,
2 Jenny Mills (c),
3 Laura Keates*,
4 Lou Dennis,
5 Rhiannon Watkins,
6 Pippa Crews,
7 Jenny Brightmore,
8 Karen Jones
*Replacements*:
16 Lucy Aylesbury,
17 Kelly Phasey,
18 Tracy Balmer*,
19 Bridget Mills*,
20 Lyndsay O'Donnell*,
21 Lauren Chenoweth
*Denotes international

# Top Flight Falcons
## Newcastle Return to the Premiership
### by CHRIS FOY

'For those at the RFU and PRL with an eye on the bigger picture, it is crucial to have a leading club serving as a beacon for aspiring young players across the far north of England'

Newcastle's promotion back to the Aviva Premiership at the first attempt in May was a cause for celebration within the corridors of power at Twickenham, as well as up on Tyneside. When the Falcons clinched the Championship title with a two-leg victory over Bedford Blues, it was a popular feat for myriad reasons, beyond the club's own ambitions and status. First and foremost, it averted the threat of English rugby enduring a drawn-out, highly public farce, for the second successive year.

Twelve months earlier, London Welsh won the Championship, having already learned that they didn't fulfil the Minimum Standards Criteria (MSC) for entry into the Premiership. Undeterred, the Exiles challenged the ruling via an RFU hearing, won their case and were belatedly promoted, amid a torrent of negative publicity for Premiership Rugby and – somewhat harshly – for the union too.

This year, Bedford had indicated a willingness to launch a similar appeal in the event of victory in the play-offs – armed with a compelling recent precedent. Thus, by beating them, Newcastle (who comfortably ticked all the MSC boxes) prevented another messy red-tape tussle.

**RIGHT** Newcastle Falcons celebrate their return to the Premiership after defeating Bedford Blues 49-33 on aggregate in the Championship play-off final.

Yet, the wider pleasure at their success was founded on so much more than a wish to preserve the credibility of the domestic game. There is a general appreciation of the Geordie club's strategic importance, as an outpost of the 15-man code in the North East. With the Premiership well represented in the West Country, London and the South East, and the Midlands, the Falcons act as a valuable presence away from the traditional heartlands.

Founded on Sir John Hall's heavy investment, they had claimed a Premiership title with a bought-in team in the early days of professionalism, but in the years that followed, their presence in the top flight was founded largely on home-grown quality. Jonny Wilkinson served as the Pied Piper and the academy churned out talented tyros: the likes of Jamie Noon, Toby Flood, Tom May and Mathew Tait. In more recent times, Geoff Parling, Phil Dowson and Lee Dickson have all made their mark with England, having been nurtured at Newcastle.

For those at the RFU and PRL with an eye on the bigger picture, it is crucial to have a leading club serving as a beacon for aspiring young players across the far north of England from Cumbria to Northumberland, and down through Durham into North Yorkshire. And with St James' Park

**ABOVE** Newcastle director of rugby Dean Richards before the Championship match at Bristol in September 2012.

**FACING PAGE** Falcons' teenage wing sensation Zach Kibirige in action for Yarm School in the final of the 2013 Daily Mail Under 18 Vase at Twickenham.

staging three matches during the 2015 World Cup, there is another reason why the authorities would welcome a resurgence by the Falcons.

That process began last season, under the assured guidance of Dean Richards – the director of rugby who was starting his own rebuilding phase after serving a three-year ban for overseeing the 'Bloodgate' controversy while in charge at Harlequins. Picking up the pieces from the relegation which occurred just before his tenure at Kingston Park began, the former England No. 8 moulded Newcastle into a formidable force from the outset.

The results were remarkable. Newcastle won 28 consecutive matches in all competitions last season until they were narrowly beaten at home by Bristol on 20 April. Having finished emphatically top of the Championship table, Richards' side suffered a scare in the first leg of their semi-final – losing at Leeds – but rallied to win on aggregate and go on to beat Bedford home and away.

While the promotion push was still ongoing, the director of rugby with a renowned Midas touch was busy assembling a squad capable of being competitive in the Premiership. There have been some shrewd acquisitions, with Andy Saull brought in from Saracens as an open-side poacher with a point to prove, scrum half Mike Blair signing from Brive to provide Test pedigree, and Noah Cato capable of providing pace and finishing prowess out wide.

Blair and Fraser McKenzie – recruited from Sale – are part of a large Scottish contingent at the club, in keeping with a long-held tradition. Others from north of the border include Scott MacLeod, Ally Hogg and Scott Lawson. They form a core of established, experienced players within the Newcastle ranks who should ensure that the club have sufficient Premiership pedigree to make a decent fist of their crusade to remain in the top division and gradually raise their horizons.

Prior to the start of the season, Richards asserted his belief that survival was a realistic objective, saying: 'I hope we don't go down; probably barring the top four or five clubs, everybody has that fear each season. It's such a tough competition and I hope we don't get sucked into a relegation battle because it is difficult to escape from. If we play as well as we can and the new guys that we have brought in gel quickly, hopefully we will have enough to stay up, I'm confident about that.'

What the Falcons may struggle with is filling the void left by Jimmy Gopperth. The Kiwi fly half left Tyneside at the end of last season for a high-profile new challenge with Leinster in Dublin, having made his name at Kingston Park as a prolific goal-kicker. Richards must hope that Rory Clegg and Phil Godman – back at the club where he served his apprenticeship before relocating to Edinburgh – can both lead the attack with conviction, even if they can't quite emulate Gopperth's point-scoring feats.

While the players brought in from elsewhere will be relied upon to lead the charge this season, for the long-term health of Newcastle and North East rugby as a whole, it is imperative that the academy resurrects the time-honoured knack for churning out rookies with abundant class. In that regard, the signs are encouraging.

Prop Scott Wilson was a member of the England Under 20 squad who won the junior World Cup in June and is a former captain at Sedburgh – the renowned rugby school. And Middlesbrough-born Zach Kibirige emerged as a teenage wing sensation last season, scoring five tries in four senior games before concentrating on his 'A' Levels. It is hoped that he will help to provide a cutting edge in harness with Cato and Alex Tait – Mathew's younger brother.

Should these youngsters continue to develop and others join them in rising to prominence, there is every chance that Newcastle will become contenders once more. With the canny Richards guiding the operation, the initial objective of Premiership survival is by no means a far-fetched one. Then he will set out to do just what he did at Quins, by plotting a course towards a future title challenge.

For now that remains a fantasy scenario, but it is one which would revitalise rugby in the region and therefore provide a positive service for English rugby as a whole.

# Peninsular Promise
## the State of West Country Rugby
### by STEVE BALE

'In this regional pecking order, it is Exeter where praise is persistently lavished, Exeter who have it within their capacity to become annual Premiership aspirants'

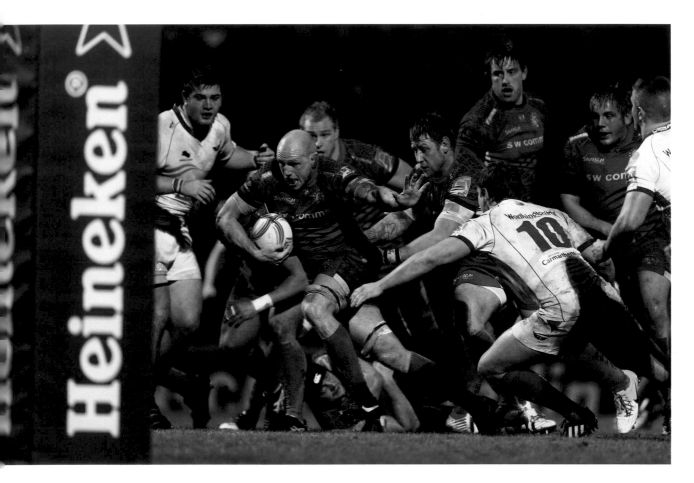

It is well within the memory of rather too many of us how the amateur era ended in the mid-1990s with Bath as the unquestioned rulers of the game in its West Country kingdom, the area of England where the game holds sway as it does nowhere else.

In view of subsequent events, not least the rise of Exeter, it is also worth recalling that the last time Bath won the domestic title, in 1995-96, Exeter too were champions, though of National Four, three tiers below the top flight.

That season Gloucester were eighth in Bath's league, Bristol sixth, while Penzance – from whom Cornish Pirates would materialise – were in the nether regions, or at any rate the eighth tier, known as Western Counties.

Bath and Gloucester are two of only four clubs who have never lost their elite status since English leagues were instituted in 1987. Leicester and Wasps are the others. Exeter have been there only since 2010, but already they stand comparison with this eminent peer group.

In fact the aspiration expressed by chairman Tony Rowe after that promotion to become a Devonian equivalent of Leicester is on its way to fruition. Heineken Cup rugby for a second successive season is only the start of it.

Sandy Park will have expanded from 10,000 to 13,000 by the time it hosts World Cup matches in 2015, and eventually Rowe intends for the ground to hold 20,000 and so give Exeter a capacity second only to Leicester's as a rugby-dedicated club venue.

The responsibility for this advance lies with Rowe to ensure the necessary funding will be in place but also with Exeter's greatly admired coach Rob Baxter to maintain the development in his team and the way they play. He knows it. 'It's still the challenge we haven't laid down to ourselves as a team or as a wider group,' said Baxter. 'What we have worked on really well is becoming a very competitive side in everything we do, in every area of our game. But maybe that should be the next step.

'We haven't talked too much about where we want to end up, where the journey we are on will take us. But we've worked really well on the blueprint and we have to ask the players what it is that will drive them over the next two or three seasons, what needs to happen to become a consistent top-four team.

'For all the progress we've made, I wouldn't say we are there yet. But this is a rugby-rich area of the country, with vast potential for Exeter. Our academy is producing some very good players. We have a very strong Under 18 group. They were unbeaten in the Premiership academy league.'

**FACING PAGE** Chiefs skipper James Scaysbrook powers to the line to score a 78th-minute try as Exeter beat the Scarlets 30-20 in the Heineken Cup at Sandy Park.

**BELOW** James Simpson-Daniel and Jim Hamilton hold up Kyle Eastmond during the Cherry and Whites' 16-10 Premiership victory over Bath at Kingsholm.

These are fundamentals, but what Baxter also has in mind is that if Exeter double the size of Sandy Park they will not get anywhere near filling it unless they repeatedly play the style of attacking rugby with which they decorated last season. So either win or occasionally lose in style.

'The way the stadium and the team have developed has worked hand in hand,' said Baxter. 'If we are to keep making this progress over the next 10 or 15 or 20 years, or even over the next five, we need to attract all these people to come and see us and then, win or lose, come back.

'You can see how we have already developed in that respect. So much of what we wanted to achieve, we have. We were more ambitious last season, targeting and scoring more tries, and still we have to keep building the complete package as a team.'

Just imagine, Exeter actually finished a place lower than in 2012. But any objective assessment is bound to conclude that in the long term, with their own ground and no developmental problems, they should at least be able to emulate whatever Gloucester do.

Bath, meanwhile, were the most professional club in amateur rugby. Those who were there at the time would probably admit they were as amateurish as any after the new dispensation of 1995 – though in England the RFU's one-year professional moratorium pointlessly delayed the dread day.

So what do we find out West today? Gloucester, fifth in the Premiership last season, were best; Exeter next in sixth. Bath's seventh place was actually a decline since Bruce Craig bought the club and they finished the 2010-11 season in fifth position.

In this regional pecking order, it is Exeter where praise is persistently lavished, Exeter whose momentum has never yet faltered, Exeter who have it within their capacity to become annual Premiership aspirants. The same ought to be said of Bath.

**RIGHT** Exiles' Joe Ajuwa claims the ball ahead of Matt Evans as London Welsh take on Cornish Pirates in the second leg of the 2012 RFU Championship play-off. Evans was on the scoresheet, but Pirates came off second best for the second year running.

**FACING PAGE** Lock Ben Glynn wins ball for Bristol against Newcastle on the opening day of the 2012-13 RFU Championship. Bristol went down 37-20 but later gained revenge on the future champions, winning 19-14 at Kingston Park.

Craig has been so dissatisfied he keeps changing the coaching set-up, his impatient expectations on arrival at the Recreation Ground three years ago unfulfilled whether it was Sir Ian McGeechan, Gary Gold or Mike Ford in charge. Still the Rec remains undeveloped. If that meant Craig was envious of Gloucester's and Exeter's self-sufficiency, he could be excused. 'From the point where I took over the club, the expectation of where we were going and how quickly was maybe exaggerated because of not necessarily understanding the depth of work needed.

'Human nature is that you are optimistic. It's frustrating – for the supporters, for the coaches, for the players, for me.'

Then there is Gloucester, and if consistency had been grafted on to the brilliance of their young back line they – rather than Exeter – would be the ones putting themselves up alongside the likes of recent title challengers Leicester, Northampton, Harlequins and Saracens.

This leaves Bristol and the Pirates with aspirations to give the Premiership still more of a West Country flavour, and while Bristol have that as a short-term aim, Cornish Pirates are trying to follow the Exeter model by developing facilities that could be worthy of a Premiership club.

But having long-awaited planning consent for a new ground outside Truro is merely a beginning and, according to Pirates proprietor Dicky Evans, it will be 2016-17 before the new home is ready. Then, though, anything is possible, bearing in mind Pirates reached the 2012 play-off final.

There they lost to London Welsh, and the Exiles' experience proved the pointlessness of promotion when you are unready – and that means as a club, never mind how good your team may be. Truro, let alone Penzance, is a fair way beyond Exeter, but the Chiefs are a standing reminder of the wisdom of planning a long way ahead.

Years ago Bristol used to have a strong Cornish connection. Nowadays there is no good reason a Cornish hopeful would look past Sandy Park. But Bristol's intention was made clear when they appointed ex-England and Scotland – and Bath – coach Andy Robinson as director of rugby.

'This is a clear indication of the burning ambition of the club,' was chairman Chris Booy's welcome to Robinson. 'He has proven experience at international and domestic level and the necessary acumen to establish us as a top-four Premiership side in the future.'

On the other hand, this is what they all say. Perhaps a word with Rob Baxter would be in order.

# Movers and Shakers
## Saracens in 2012-13

### by TERRY COOPER

'When you think about it, a sports stadium is a useless waste of money for all but a couple of hours a fortnight – but not where we play'

Savage disappointment – not dejection or despair – was the main reaction by Saracens after they were eliminated in two major semi-finals last spring. But in the grand scheme of rugby progress the season must be put in the file labelled 'Success'.

Saracens' long-serving figurehead, chairman Nigel Wray, who has guided the club from prominence to elite status since the early months of professionalism, rightly boasted: 'We secured, for the very first time in our history, the top position in the Premiership at the end of the regular season.'

And he wants to know why there is no trophy for coming top after the 22-game slog. Well, there used to be, but the actual cup for that marathon feat was an infant toddler compared with the vast prize that the winners of the two-match sprint play-off received.

Wray adds: 'Even more important than a single playing triumph was finally creating our own ground, with its all-weather pitch, at Allianz Park after 17 years of being at the mercy of the owner or landlord of somebody else's ground.

'And I have doubts that, without that pitch, we would not have got planning permission anywhere in London. The local council would not have given us approval to take over Barnet Copthall Stadium if we had not committed to the artificial-grass pitch, with massive amounts of rubber under the surface. That means *no more mud* and is available to several hundred local school-children, who compete each week in all sorts of sports on a pitch used by a professional club. No more postponed matches for us or cancelled games-days for kids of the local borough.

It was a major triumph becoming a home-owner. Not owning your home ground is like having someone else's family photos on display in your front room.

'When you think about it, a sports stadium is a useless waste of money for all but a couple of hours a fortnight – but not where we play.

'All the visiting fans have told me how wonderful and family-friendly our stadium is. Even Northampton supporters congratulated us. They have their own new stadium and a family atmosphere, so they know what they are talking about. And Cardiff Blues, who were the first visitors to tread the new surface, have decided that they will have an artificial pitch. These are compliments from two of the oldest British clubs.'

Director of rugby Mark McCall is a devotee of the green, green 'grass' of Home – At Last. And he has his own slogan: 'We can invite fans to "stay *on* the pitch".'

'The surface creates a faster, safer and more entertaining game all year round. When the rest of the country is covered in snow or ankle deep in water we can train and play on a perfect surface.'

**FACING PAGE** Saracens and Cardiff Blues compete in a line out during their LV= Cup match in January 2013, the first professional game to take place at Allianz Park.

**BELOW** Chris Ashton of Saracens is tackled by Leicester's Geoff Parling (left) and Sam Harrison in last season's Aviva Premiership 9-9 draw at Wembley. Sarries finished top of the table but slipped up in the play-offs, and Leicester claimed the prize.

What peace of mind a coach must get when he is guaranteed that his midweek training schedule is not going to be disrupted by flood or frost, while other coaches are texting their squads to head for the nearest gym.

Wray laments the shortfalls when the heat came on in those semi-finals. 'Our most consistent display was against Ulster in the quarter-final and if we had played like that against Northampton and Toulon we might have won.

'If we had been told that we would get to two semi-finals we would have said that would have been good. But to lose both was frustrating.

'In those semis we look back and see that we conceded 17 points in seven minutes against Northampton. That was an extraordinarily bad spell. We had beaten them twice in the Premiership. Toulon were also eminently beatable, as was proved in the closest possible Heineken Cup final and losing in their Top 14 play-off.'

Saracens began a smooth Heineken campaign by thumping always dangerous Edinburgh 45-0 at Murrayfield. In Brussels they beat Racing Métro 30-13. In December they pinched a bonus point in Limerick, but Munster grabbed their own bonus a week later. The key result was beating Racing in Nantes and sealing the deal with another 40-pointer against Edinburgh. Ulster was a highlight, but then Jonny and his left boot arrived at Twickenham to crush the life out of Farrell, his England successor, and Saracens. But then Jonny has been doing that to opponents for more than a decade.

When Wray acquired the club, they were playing on their traditional park pitch at Southgate. He effected a temporary, one-season transfer to Enfield FC. In 1997 they switched to Watford's ground at Vicarage Road, which was at least a sports stadium. It deteriorated sadly, with threequarters of one stand condemned and deserted. Around the time of the move to Hertfordshire, Wray said: 'I have a vision of us playing a Heineken Cup quarter-final in front of a packed Vicarage Road against one of the glamour French teams, like Toulouse.'

Well, they did play a home quarter-final at Allianz Park against Ulster. Not a star French outfit, but Ulster were once Heineken Cup winners and were 2012 finalists.

**LEFT** Olly Barkley and Jacques Cronje cannot prevent Sarries captain Steve Borthwick touching down against Racing Métro in the 2012-13 Heineken Cup. Saracens played this home pool-stage game at the King Baudouin Stadium in Brussels.

Wray cannot control results, much as he plans, dreams and visualises. But even he was confronted with an unexpected Sarries moment while running up a London Underground escalator recently. His eye was caught by the repeating advertisements on the wall posted by a TV company for forthcoming attractions. They featured famous sportsmen. 'I glanced at Robin van Persie, then Owen Farrell, then van Persie, more Farrell and so on, alternately, right to the top. For a rugby player to get the same billing as van Persie was interesting.'

Perhaps it was a sign of the future – Saracens buying a ticket and ascending the escalator right to the top. Chief executive Ed Griffiths comments: 'I believe that 2012-13 was a fantastic success, especially when you look at the long-term trend over the last four years. We have been consistently competitive in both the Heineken Cup and the Premiership, with a quarter-final and now a semi-final in Europe and table-toppers this season after being domestic champions two years ago.

'It's all moving in the right direction. Admittedly, though, when you reach two semi-finals you have to hope or expect one winning outcome. So that was undeniably disappointing.

'At the start of the year we played the first of six games at Allianz Park in Hendon and had sell-out crowds of 10,000 including almost full take-up of hospitality. Generally, it is clubs who own their ground that are commercially successful.

'After some years of chop and change in the coaching department, we hope to have found a longer-term Rugby Director in the highly regarded Mark McCall, and Paul Gustard emulated some of our players by going to Argentina as part of the England coaching team.

'We have some South African players, but, to balance that, we have brought through about half a dozen men who have reached England's EPS squad. People talk as though we are full of big-name players, but we have bought only four established internationals: Chris Ashton, David Strettle, Charlie Hodgson and Richard Wigglesworth.

'Other star names like Mako Vunipola, Owen Farrell, Alex Goode and Brad Barritt and most of the rest of the squad have developed and improved over the last four years just by being here.'

There's much more than public-relations platitudes when the players discuss their club. Take Owen Farrell: 'They do things out of the box here. For instance, there's never a normal team meeting. The stats-chart for defence is known as the "Wolf Board" and the forwards call themselves "The Wolf Pack". So what did the coaches do at one meeting? They brought in a couple of real, live wolves. I was pretty nervous.'

All rugby players have encountered a coach who acts like a foaming, half-mad, raging wild animal, so Farrell should not have been surprised, especially given the coaches' record. Gustard and Alex Sanderson have introduced a small crocodile, a tarantula and a few snakes into meetings on the principle that most of what they say goes in one ear and out the other, but with wild animals hovering the message might have a big impact. Perhaps the coaches should have brought a python into the changing room before the Heineken semi-final to show the boys what Jonny could do in the crushing-the-life-out-of-you department. No rugby players were harmed during these meetings.

Farrell continues: 'We're a tight-knit group, all about putting your body on the line for each other.' And captain Steve Borthwick: 'We are not treated just as players. We are managed as human beings. We are a social club that plays rugby. We've been taken to Verbier, the Munich Beer Festival and Miami. We are odd, but that's just what we are.

'Topping the Premiership was special – but we want to be European champions and it will come.'

Saracens have been the target of many criticisms – tedious, defensive – but all clubs would envy their achievements last season. They finished a clear three points ahead of Leicester in the Premiership, and their 17 wins were two more than the Tigers managed. There was one draw and a mere four defeats. Something was working all season long, until the knockout meltdown.

And finally. Allianz Park was named Small Venue of the Year at the annual Stadium Business Summit Awards. Well, if you can't win the Heineken or the Premiership at least get on the podium. I sincerely trust that there was a massive prize for this honour. The judges said: 'It's a brave move to put in turf for rugby and other sports but it has proved to be the key to more pitch-use. This is the kind of small venue with "big ideas" that we like – engaging with the local and international community.'

Saracens have also been shortlisted for the Beyond Sport Club of the Year Award, competing against 350 applicants from around the world.

# The Rules Rule
## the 2012-13 Aviva Premiership
### by CHRIS HEWETT

*'Off Hartley trudged, ashen-faced with good reason. Not only had he left his side at the mercy of the Tigers, but he had also kissed goodbye to a treasured place in the Lions party'*

O ften in recent years – too often, perhaps – the dramatic crux at the end of the Premiership's long round-robin phase has occurred at the bottom of the table rather than the top: something which never fails to bemuse rugby folk in the southern hemisphere, unfamiliar as they are with the pain and trauma of relegation in top-level competition. More than one former Wallaby international has been heard to wonder aloud why the fuddy-duddy

***ABOVE*** Manu Tuilagi of Leicester runs away from the Saints defence to score the Tigers' third try in the 2013 Aviva Premiership final at Twickenham.

English and the peculiar French seem more interested in the also-rans than the pacesetters when the important issues are decided in mid-spring.

Last season, the Premiership was spared its annual outbreak of last-weekend paranoia, for London Welsh were already on the wrong side of the arithmetic by then. Yet in many ways, they were still the story of the campaign. Rather like Basil Fawlty's infamous moose's head, they were up … and then they were down again. And in between times, they caused no end of trouble.

Promoted in controversial, not to say long-winded circumstances after winning an appeal against the Rugby Football Union's initial rejection of their top-flight credentials – if they could not boast the strongest team in rugby terms, the Exiles had one hell of a line-up when it came to legal argument – the men from Old Deer Park were confidently expected to be off the back of the Premiership peloton, to confuse sports just for a second, by the end of November. As it turned out, they reached Christmas in the rudest of health after four excellent league victories (which was four more than many had anticipated): indeed, even the darkest-minded of Jeremiahs began to wonder whether they might turn logic on its head and successfully defend their top-flight status.

This would have been nothing short of miraculous, given the brutal disadvantages they had faced in piecing together a competitive team almost from scratch and then playing their home games in the unfamiliar surroundings of the Kassam Stadium in Oxford. That Lyn Jones, their wonderfully resourceful head coach, managed to take them as close to survival as he did was, in itself, a terrific feat of ingenuity. Had they stayed up, someone would have presented him with a shirt bearing the name 'Merlin' (who, according to legend, may well have been Welsh!).

Inevitably, they could not maintain their form when many of their most important players – the hard-tackling centre Hudson Tonga'uiha, the inexhaustibly energetic hooker-cum-flanker Neil Briggs, the strongman scrummager Franck Montanella, the skilful young No. 8 Ed Jackson … even the celebrity outside half Gavin Henson, who produced some terrific rugby on the rare occasions he took the field – broke down with injury, leaving Jones with scant resources. And when scandal broke, they were in no position to rise above it.

And what a sorry scandal it was: no more than a minor misdemeanour compared with the fake blood affair at Harlequins four years previously, but of sufficient magnitude to force the RFU into a stern defence of the league's integrity. The scrum half Tyson Keats, a New Zealander, was found to have played a significant number of pre-Christmas games on false papers filed to the authorities by the Exiles' team manager Mike Scott. Keats was in no way to blame – Scott was judged wholly

responsible and banned from all rugby involvement for life – and the club argued that they too were innocent victims of a single individual's malfeasance. Not even London Welsh's lawyers could swing that one, though. Five precious Premiership points were docked and their goose was cooked.

So it was that the other strugglers, Sale and London Irish, finished a difficult season in more comfortable circumstances than might otherwise have been the case. Sale had signed a celebrity outside half of their own in Danny Cipriani, back in England after a spell of Super 15 rugby with the Melbourne Rebels and keen to show the new Red Rose management team headed by Stuart Lancaster that he was not quite the wayward soul of popular imagination. It did not work out for him: by the end of the campaign, he was no better than second choice at No. 10, and when he hit the headlines, it was for being clobbered by a bus during an end-of-season pub crawl with his clubmates. 'He must be seriously slow if he can't sidestep something moving that slowly,' muttered Steve Diamond, his rugby director, sardonically.

London Irish, back under the stewardship of Brian Smith following the Australian's three-year stint as England's attack coach, were an odd lot. Their outstanding loose-head prop Alex Corbisiero played precious little rugby; the Test centre Jonathan Joseph did not quite kick on after a strong 2011-12 campaign; Jamie Gibson, their bright young thing in the back row, failed to fulfil expectations. By the end of the season, all three had announced plans to move on – to Northampton, Bath and Leicester respectively – leaving the Madejski Stadium crowd wondering just what the future might hold.

At the other end of the table, the usual suspects gathered at the top: Harlequins, the holders, and Saracens, the 2011 champions, were

*FACING PAGE* Mathew Tait, the Leicester full back, gives Nick Evans and Nick Easter of Harlequins the slip during the Tigers' 33-16 semi-final victory at Welford Road.

*BELOW* The Saracens defence get to grips with Soane Tonga'uiha but could not stop Northampton running out 27-13 winners in their semi-final at Allianz Park.

always good bets for a play-off finish, as were ultra-consistent Leicester, by whom any keen student of the Premiership can happily set his watch. At various points, Gloucester, invigorated by the coaching of Nigel Davies and blessed with a blossoming midfield relationship between Freddie Burns and Billy Twelvetrees, seemed likely to join the big boys. So, briefly, did a Wasps team lovingly nursed back to life by their rugby director David Young and featuring some unusually talented youngsters: the wing Christian Wade, the utility back Elliot Daly, the lock Joe Launchbury and the No. 8 Billy Vunipola among them.

But when push came to shove, it was Northampton who shoved hardest and elbowed their way into the semi-finals. They had not been wholly convincing – having lost two influential players, the centre James Downey and the No. 8 Roger Wilson, to Irish provincial rugby at the end of the previous season, they suffered for their failure to replace like with like – but they were always capable of delivering a one-off performance. That much was clear when they won a Heineken Cup match on the road in Belfast before Christmas: until then, Ulster had appeared next to unbeatable at Ravenhill.

So it was that the Saints travelled to Saracens on semi-final day and ransacked Allianz Park, where the Londoners had not looked like losing a game since moving there from Vicarage Road. Samu Manoa, a United States international flanker of Tongan descent, had the mother and father of a barnstormer that afternoon – if such battle-hardened Sarries forwards as Matt Stevens and Steve Borthwick ever see him again, it will be many years too soon – and with Dylan Hartley leading from the front in characteristically confrontational style, the victory was as complete as it had been unforeseen.

With the other semi-final being played at Welford Road, precious few people predicted anything other than a Leicester victory, even though Harlequins were not the sorts to be fazed by a trip to English club rugby's most intimidating venue. Sure enough, the runes were read correctly: Quins gave it a very decent shot and were probably the better side in the first half, but they contrived to present the Tigers with a soft try by refusing – or, maybe, forgetting – to kick the ball off the field with the interval beckoning, and from there on in, the reinvigorated Mathew Tait ran them ragged from full back. Quins will not necessarily agree, but one of the principal pleasures of the season was the return to form of Tait, perhaps the richest attacking talent to emerge in England since the turn

**ABOVE** Saints hooker and skipper Dylan Hartley talks with Jim Mallinder after being red-carded during the Aviva Premiership final at Twickenham.

of the new century. If he can rediscover enough of the best of himself to force his way back into international rugby in time for the World Cup in 2015, Lancaster and his colleagues will not be the losers by it.

Sadly, what promised to be the most interesting of 'derby' finals – Leicester against their nearest and dearest from Northampton – was cruelly and exasperatingly distorted by events at the end of the first half. Hartley, as pumped-up as ever, had already been warned for making choice comments in the heat of battle: Wayne Barnes, the referee, informed him that if he thought such remarks were aimed in his direction, he would be forced to 'deal with it'. A few minutes later, after the outside half Stephen Myler had himself ignored Barnes's advice by booting a restart straight into touch, Hartley was heard to use the word 'cheat', preceded by a short epithet of Anglo-Saxon provenance. The referee took it personally, reached for his red card and sent the hooker from the field.

Off Hartley trudged, ashen-faced with good reason. Not only had he left his side at the mercy of the Tigers, who were just about as merciless as it gets in smearing their depleted opponents all over Twickenham, but he had also kissed goodbye to a treasured place in the Lions party for the Test series in Australia. It was a heavy price to pay for a two-second outburst, but in a season of expensive misjudgments – relegation will cost London Welsh a veritable mint – it was of a piece. Rugby may have changed to the point of unrecognisability since the end of the amateur era, but it's still a good idea to stay within the law. The rules rule, even now.

# Young Quins Win
## the 2012-13 LV= Cup

### by PAUL BOLTON

'Williams crossed on the overlap after Twomey, who is still an academy player, won a line out; Guest then picked up and drove from a five-metre scrum'

The LV= Cup promised to be the first leg of a glorious treble for Harlequins when they won the competition for the first time in 22 years; instead it turned out to be a consolation prize in a season of near misses. A home defeat by Munster in the Heineken Cup quarter-finals ended Harlequins' European dreams, and their defence of the Aviva Premiership ended with a semi-final loss to eventual champions Leicester at Welford Road.

*BELOW* Harlequins No. 8 Tom Guest drives for the line to score his side's second try of the LV= Cup final, despite the efforts of the Sale defence.

Harlequins won the LV= Cup with almost a second-string side, intelligently captained by Luke Wallace, although their England contingent of Chris Robshaw, Mike Brown, Joe Marler and Danny Care were at Worcester's Sixways Stadium to watch the final, 24 hours after they missed out on a Six Nations Grand Slam in Cardiff.

'A lot of the fellas out there have to do a lot of donkey work in the training sessions for the senior players so it was nice for them to repay the favour the other way,' said Conor O'Shea, the Harlequins director of rugby.

Just as pleasing for O'Shea was that 14 members of Harlequins' squad for the final were aged 23 or under and had progressed from the successful academy system at the Stoop. 'For the club not only is it a major trophy but when you look at Sam Twomey, Charlie Matthews, Will Collier and Rob Buchanan they are five guys in our tight five who are 21 or under,' O'Shea said.

'That's something for them to store away in the locker for years to come. They are the cornerstone of what this club will be about for a decade or more.

'We told them before not to take anything for granted because you never know when you are going to get here.'

Harlequins backed up victory against a more experienced Bath side in the semi-finals with another energetic performance, but it was Tom Williams and Tom Guest, two of the older heads in their side, who helped to break Sale's resistance with first-half tries. Williams crossed on the overlap after Twomey, who is still an academy player, won a line out; Guest then picked up and drove from a five-metre scrum after Sale had struggled to cope with Ben Botica's grubber kick.

The try that decided a one-sided final came five minutes into the second half, when centre Tom Casson cut a perfect angle from a line out and left a trail of tacklers in his wake on a diagonal run to the line. It threatened to become a rout when Wallace crossed from close range, and Sale supporters were singing 'Always Look on the Bright Side of Life' long before Johnny Leota clawed back a consolation try for them.

League survival was always the priority for Sale, but their outstanding form in the cup, which included wins over Saracens in the pool stage and again in the semi-finals, helped to transform their season. 'We came over here to give it our best shot and we're pleased with the effort but our skill-set let us down,' said Sale director of rugby Steve Diamond.

'This has always been a bit of fantasy for us, we played really well in the pool stage, we beat Saracens twice to get here and we've had a great day out, so there are a lot of good, positive things.'

Sale reached the final of the competition for the first time in nine years by beating Saracens 21-15 in the semi-finals. A Sunday lunchtime kick-off and bitterly cold weather deterred all but the most loyal supporters, but those who braved the elements were rewarded with a tense semi-final which saw Sale edge through thanks to a late try from replacement scrum half Nathan Fowles followed by a penalty from Danny Cipriani.

Tom Williams scored a brace of tries in Harlequins' 31-23 win over Bath in their semi-final at the Stoop, but it was Ben Botica's penalty in an 11-point haul for the fly half, the son of former All Black Frano, that put victory beyond Bath and denied them a place in the final. Botica finished as the leading points scorer in the competition with 78, five ahead of Cipriani.

Harlequins also beat Bath (21-12) in a pool match at the Stoop in the second round of matches in December and were deserved champions as they were the only side to go through the competition unbeaten.

Sale's only defeat in the pool stage came in their opening match against London Irish at the Madejski Stadium, but Charlie Amesbury's late try helped them to salvage a valuable losing bonus point. Cipriani then scored 21 points in a 36-17 home win over Scarlets, and a thrilling 33-30 win which inflicted a first home defeat of the season on Wasps clinched Sale's place in the semi-finals.

The competition was the eighth to follow the Anglo-Welsh format, although the system of sides from Pools One and Four and teams in Pools Two and Three playing each other dates from the 2009-10 competition.

# THE BRITISH & IRISH LIONS
## WILL SAIL AGAIN...

From 1888 to today the Legend of THE BRITISH & IRISH LIONS
continues to grow. Relive the *epic journey* of the victorious
BRITISH & IRISH LIONS on **HSBC's** *interactive* **YouTube channel**.

youtube.com/LionsHSBC

After wins by the Ospreys in 2008 and Cardiff Blues in 2009, this was the fourth consecutive all-English final. This time the four Welsh sides made little impression on the tournament and managed just seven wins between them, including a 22-16 win for the Scarlets over Cardiff Blues at Parc y Scarlets in November.

London Welsh, whose focus was always going to be on attempting to stay in the Aviva Premiership, failed to win a match or collect a point in their first season in the competition, which was followed by relegation. The Exiles conceded 40 points in three of their four pool matches, with a 23-6 defeat by Harlequins at the Stoop in January representing their 'best' effort.

Saracens showed initiative by taking their opening match against Leicester, the defending champions, to Bedford's Goldington Road and were rewarded with a 3000 crowd on a chilly November evening and a 38-21 win against a mostly second-string Tigers.

Saracens then made history by staging their second home match of the tournament, against Cardiff Blues, at their new headquarters at Allianz Park in Barnet, the game being played on their state-of-the-art rubber-crumb pitch. The match took place in front of a restricted 3726 attendance and was used as a successful dress rehearsal for Saracens' opening league fixture at the ground against Exeter three weeks later. Saracens won 19-11, but Cardiff were so impressed with the artificial pitch that they decided to install one themselves at the Arms Park.

Leicester's title defence picked up after their opening-round defeat: they beat London Irish and Wasps at Welford Road but were then beaten 40-19 by Scarlets at Parc y Scarlets, by which time Sale had already won the pool.

The 35 matches produced an aggregate attendance of 266,587, with the Leicester v Wasps pool match at Welford Road attracting the biggest crowd of 19,757.

*BELOW* Skipper Luke Wallace and his Harlequins team celebrate victory in the 2013 LV= Cup final at Sixways.

# Jonny of Toulon
# the 2012-13 Heineken
# Cup

## by DAVID HANDS

'Once Wilkinson had landed the angled conversion, Toulon were a point to the good, and though a quarter-hour remained, Clermont could find no way through'

It may have been an all-French final, the fourth such in the 18-year history of the Heineken Cup and by far the best of that quartet, but for one Englishman in particular it was a day unlike any he had known in a long and utterly distinguished career.

In the evening of his playing career, Jonny Wilkinson at last placed his hands around the trophy for Europe's premier club competition. Wilkinson, who turned 34 a few days after the final, may have experienced everything that international rugby could throw at him, but his club cupboard was virtually bare before he nursed Toulon to their 16-15 win over Clermont Auvergne at Dublin's Aviva Stadium. His 12 years at Newcastle Falcons allowed him to be a relative bystander when the club won the Allied Dunbar Premiership in 1998: back then the Falcons had Rob Andrew playing fly half and kicking goals. Wilkinson did both when Newcastle beat Harlequins in the 2001 Tetley's Bitter Cup final, but when he left for Toulon in 2009, many felt it to be a move away from the northeast he should have made far earlier.

Hence the broad grin across his face when Toulon stole away from Dublin with a match they seemed certain to lose just after half-time. Within the course of eight minutes Napolioni Nalaga (the tournament's leading try scorer with eight) scored Clermont's first try and Brock James scored a second to put the favourites 15-6 ahead. But throughout the knockout phase, Clermont had demonstrated a timidity when going for the jugular and they did so now. Wilkinson knocked over his third penalty goal and when Juan-Martín Fernández Lobbe forced a turnover at a maul, Delon Armitage found himself with a big blind side and no one in his way on a 40-metre canter to the line.

Armitage, of course, was another Englishman with something to celebrate, along with Andrew Sheridan (once of Sale Sharks), Nick Kennedy and, from the bench, Steffon Armitage, who like his older brother and Kennedy formerly played for London Irish. Delon Armitage found himself the subject of some overblown criticism for his gesture in waving bye-bye to James en route to the line; unnecessary, yes, but Armitage is a player of his time and no one said a word after Mike Phillips did something similar when scoring for the British & Irish Lions against the Barbarians a fortnight later.

Once Wilkinson had landed the angled conversion, Toulon were a point to the good, and though a quarter-hour remained, Clermont could find no way through. The statistics tell the tale of where they foundered: despite enjoying 75 per cent of the territory and 68 per cent possession, they met an uncompromising defence in which Toulon made 176 tackles compared with a meagre 66 from Clermont. Remarkably Carl Hayman, the New Zealand prop, led the tackle count with 17, two more tight forwards, Fernández Lobbe and Kennedy, made 15 and 11 respectively and Joe van Niekerk made nine in the 30 minutes he was on the pitch. No Clermont player made more than eight tackles.

Inevitably Wilkinson was named European Player of the Year little more than 24 hours after the final and, almost equally inevitably, Toulon could not replicate their success in France's Top 14 final two weeks later, where they lost to Castres. But Wilkinson's contribution to his club's Heineken success, as captain and goal-kicker, was not confined to the final: in the three knockout games of the tournament he scored 56 of Toulon's 61 points and ended the European season with 108 points from all cup games.

'All of a sudden you can appreciate the World Cup in a way I've never done,' Wilkinson said, referring to the 2003 final in which his extra-time dropped goal earned England the Webb Ellis Cup against

**FACING PAGE** Familiar style, familiar result. Jonny Wilkinson knocks over the 65th-minute conversion that proved the match-winning score in the final at the Aviva Stadium.

**BELOW** Delon Armitage runs in Toulon's try in Dublin, waving to Brock James as he goes.

Australia in Sydney. '2003 was great but it was almost battling me every time I stepped on to the field, trying to show me up. This victory is like the World Cup but in a way more special as it is with the guys I am with day in, day out.'

That Toulon won the Heineken Cup with a starting XV including only four Frenchmen is a matter for concern within domestic circles, but few would question the commitment of players drawn to the Mediterranean port by Mourad Boudjellal's cash. Indeed, 13 countries were represented in the playing squads of the two finalists, and Clermont's coach, Vern Cotter from New Zealand, was named a few days later as Scotland's new head coach.

Such diversity may help the organisers sell television coverage to more than 150 countries, but the future of the competition remained up in the air going into the 2013-14 season, the last under the existing accord. Hours before the 2013 final in Dublin, representatives of the six competing countries were invited to a meeting organised by Pierre Camou, president of the French Rugby Federation, and intended to head off the breakaway of the leading clubs in England and France.

That shadow hung over the 2012-13 season like a shroud, a succession of meetings failing to find an acceptable answer. Meanwhile, the players, as is their wont, got on with what they do best – playing rugby; and the early pool stages suggested that this could well be France's year. Toulouse, for example, battered Leicester on the opening weekend, and Racing Métro put paid to Munster in Paris.

But both Leicester and Munster, past European champions, have learned how to play the long game and it was they who reached the last eight whereas Racing and Toulouse, the competition's most successful club, did not. It is worth remembering, too, that even though there was an all-French final involving Toulon and Clermont, that success was not reflected in the RBS Six Nations Championship, where France finished bottom of the heap (a year earlier Ireland's form was not dissimilar, despite Leinster's European success).

*RIGHT* Clermont Auvergne left wing Napolioni Nalaga, the leading try scorer in the 2012-13 Heineken Cup competition, squeezes in at the corner for his side's first touchdown of the final, despite the efforts of Delon Armitage.

And what of Leinster, the 2012 champions? They were given something of a hurry-up at the Royal Dublin Society Showgrounds by those newcomers to the Heineken Cup, Exeter Chiefs. It was a remarkable display by the Chiefs, who deserved at least a draw but had to settle for a 9-6 defeat – yet the expectation was that the Irish province would get their act together and defend their title with tenacity.

But Leinster were in the same pool as Clermont, and the French club proved an insurmountable obstacle. In deep December they won 15-12 at the Stade Marcel Michelin, not a try in sight, and a week later carried off a 28-21 win over Leinster at the Aviva Stadium. A try by Wesley Fofana and the accuracy of Morgan Parra's boot embellished Clermont's power at the set-piece and condemned Leinster to the knockout phase of the Amlin Challenge Cup (which they duly won).

The main English challenge for honours appeared to reside initially with Saracens and Harlequins. During a nomadic first half of their season, Saracens took their 'home' game against Racing Métro to the King Baudouin Stadium in Brussels, where they were rewarded with an 18,000 crowd and a 30-13 win, but they came adrift – as so many others have done – against a resurgent Munster, losing 15-9 at Thomond Park.

Northampton endured a topsy-turvy season from start to finish, but they will always cherish their 2012 trip to Belfast. The previous weekend they had been battered by Ulster on their own patch, but they stood strong at Ravenhill to win 10-9 and take away Ulster's hitherto unbeaten record.

It was not enough to see them through to the quarter-finals, but the final fortnight of pool qualification ensured Northampton were not the only famous name to depart the competition. Leicester did the most damage, first by drawing 15-15 with the Ospreys at the Liberty Stadium and denying any Welsh representation in the last eight, then a week later by beating Toulouse 9-5 in a tumultuous clash at a snowy Welford Road.

Toulon themselves received a bloody nose in losing 23-3 at Montpellier, which earned the victors the dubious privilege of a quarter-final at Clermont. The two countries, England and France, who had served notice the previous summer of their intention to quit the Heineken Cup in its existing format, ended with three quarter-finalists each, while Ireland provided the other two, Munster and Ulster.

The toughest task was that of Leicester, who travelled to Toulon in April boosted by the revival in domestic form which was to carry them all the way to the Aviva Premiership title. They might have prevailed had they not played a quarter of the match with 14 men, Dan Cole and Toby Flood receiving yellow cards after Flood had pushed Leicester into a 9-0 lead with three penalties.

Since they also lost Marcos Ayerza, the Argentine prop, with a broken collarbone after a controversial challenge by Bakkies Botha, Leicester felt justifiably aggrieved at a 21-15 defeat. They had far more cause for complaint than Harlequins, who fell completely flat at the Twickenham Stoop against Munster and lost 18-12, a Munster moreover with the returning Paul O'Connell back at something like his rampaging best.

O'Connell, the Ireland lock, missed the Six Nations while recovering from an operation to a bulging disc in his back, but this was the start of his journey towards Lions selection. Over the road at the main Twickenham Stadium 24 hours earlier, Ulster were not so fortunate: they found Saracens (coached by former Ulster centre Mark McCall) in unforgiving mood, and tries by Will Fraser and Chris Ashton put paid to their hopes.

Clermont, 36-14 victors over Montpellier, were at home again in the semi-final with Munster and needed every slice of domestic advantage. The scoring sequence presaged that of the final, since Clermont took a 16-3 lead early in the second half thanks to a wonderful try from Nalaga and Parra's goal-kicking. But Munster, under the cosh in so many areas, clung on, Denis Hurley scored a try and Clermont were relieved to come away with a 16-10 win.

Wilkinson, meanwhile, took his Toulon team back to familiar stamping grounds. Twickenham hosted the other semi-final, which became a case of master v pupil – Wilkinson against Owen Farrell, now the occupant of England's No. 10 shirt, which had for so long been Wilkinson's. The winner was not in doubt: where Farrell flickered from darkness to light and back again, Wilkinson was magisterial, one moment capturing the difference.

With Toulon leading 18-12, Wilkinson squeezed out a dropped goal under the onrushing Farrell's body. As the two men picked themselves off the ground, Wilkinson patted the youngster on the back, not in any sense of superiority but a 'better luck next time' gesture, beautifully captured by the television camera. Saracens had their chances but could not take them; Wilkinson, in probably his last match at Twickenham, kicked seven penalties to go with his drop and led Toulon to their 24-12 win and their first Heineken Cup final.

# Leinster's Euro Double
## the 2012-13 Amlin Challenge Cup by IAN ROBERTSON

'Leinster had much the better of the first half and they scored three wonderful tries through Ian Madigan, Sean Cronin and Rob Kearney. Jonny Sexton converted all three'

The seventeenth Amlin Challenge Cup final produced two teams, Leinster and Stade Français, who were each playing in this great event for the first time. Not surprisingly with two of the very best teams in Europe each renowned for their fervent supporters, the game attracted a capacity crowd. They were duly rewarded as the RDS Arena hosted one of the very best Amlin Cup finals.

It was not only a great occasion, it was also a great match. Despite the big margin of victory (34-13 to Leinster) it was a game not just of enormous intensity but also one of consummate skill.

Full credit to Stade Français, who could have been forgiven if they had embarked on a damage-limitation exercise when they were 21-3 down approaching half-time, but instead they played their full part in joining in a wonderful game of high-octane free-flowing rugby.

It was a great end to the season and underlined the huge benefit of the Amlin Cup system, which encourages the concept of the best losing Heineken Cup pool teams joining the winning pool sides from the Amlin Cup at the quarter-final stage. This

**FACING PAGE** Leinster inside centre Ian Madigan runs away to score his side's first try after just two minutes.

**ABOVE** Sergio Parisse, Stade's Italian skipper, is gang-tackled by the Leinster defence.

**RIGHT** Joe Schmidt added the Amlin Challenge Cup to his two Heineken triumphs at Leinster before moving on to become Ireland coach. The province also won the RaboDirect title in 2012-13.

guarantees a very high standard of teams in the knockout stages of the Amlin Cup and this resulted in the tremendous final in Dublin.

When you consider that Leinster have won the European Cup three times in the last four years, it was no surprise they started clear favourites to win the final in their home city of Dublin. Indeed Leinster became only the fourth team to win both the Amlin Cup and Heineken Cup. The other three clubs to achieve this elusive double are Bath, Wasps and Northampton.

Leinster had much the better of the first half and they scored three wonderful tries through Ian Madigan, Sean Cronin and Rob Kearney. Jonny Sexton converted all three.

In the second half Sexton continued in good form, kicking two more penalties and converting the final try of the match, scored by Cian Healy in the very last minute. Stade Français entered into the spirit of the match and they were rewarded with a try by Jérémy Sinzelle. It was very refreshing to see two teams embrace the challenge of running the ball, with all the risks that entailed, to produce such a memorable match.

It is also important to acknowledge the success of the relatively new arrangement of playing both the Amlin Cup and the Heineken Cup finals in the same city and on the same weekend. This makes for a great rugby weekend, with the Amlin Cup on the Friday night and the Heineken Cup on the Saturday. It bodes well for the future of both these excellent competitions.

And two footnotes: Two people deserve special mention for their part in helping to make this match so special. First, Joe Schmidt, who has enjoyed great success with Leinster in recent seasons and who has now moved on to be the coach of Ireland. There is no doubt he is out of the top drawer. So too is referee Nigel Owens, who deserved praise for his tremendous handling of the match.

**RIGHT** Rob Kearney, Leinster's Ireland and Lions full back, evades his Stade Français opposite number Jérôme Porical to score his side's third try.

**PAGES 112-113** A jubilant Leinster join the select club of sides that have won both European titles, after beating Stade Français 34-13 to lift the Amlin Challenge Cup for 2012-13.

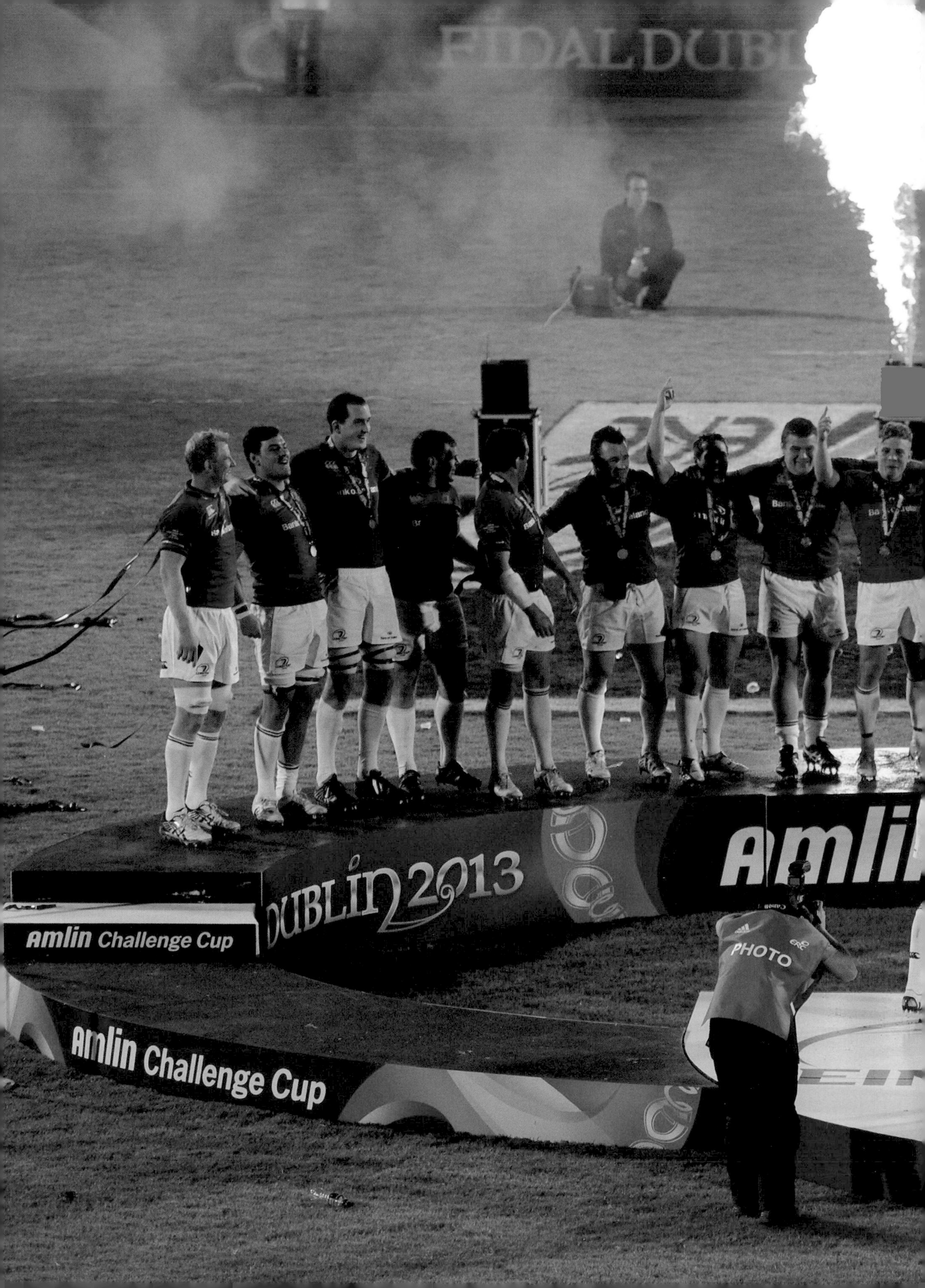

DUBLIN 2013
Amlin Challenge Cup
Amlin Challenge Cup
PHOTO

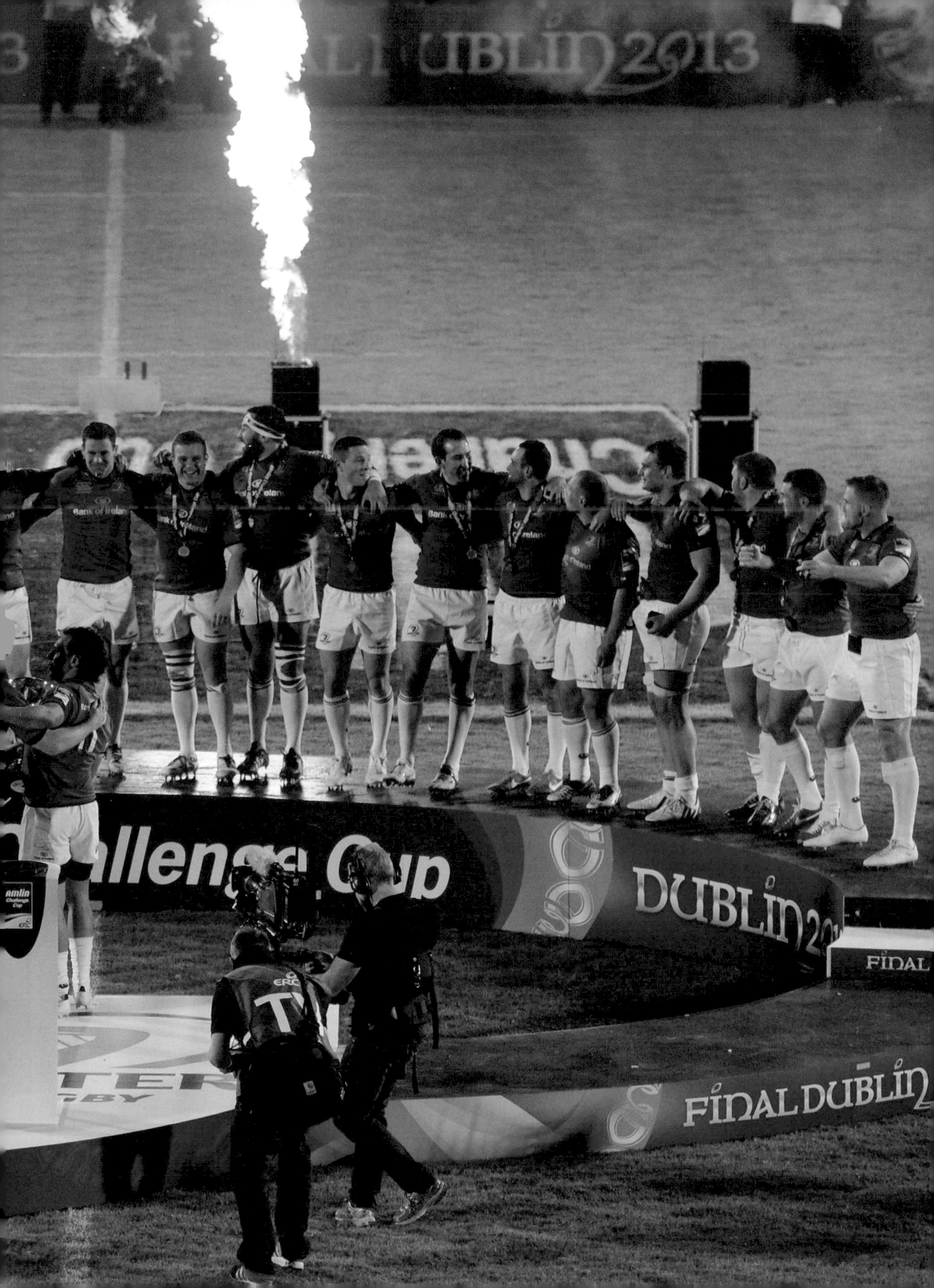
UBLIN 2013
allenge Cup
DUBLIN
FINAL DUBLIN

Congratulations to **Leinster Rugby**
Amlin Challenge Cup Champions 2013

Amlin is proud to be supporting the Wooden Spoon book 2014

www.amlin.com

# REVIEW OF THE
# SEASON 2012-13

# Wales Humble England
## the 2013 Six Nations Championship

by **CHRIS JONES**

'It was the first time since 1979 that Wales had successfully defended a Five or Six Nations title, and Howley was able to savour a notable triumph'

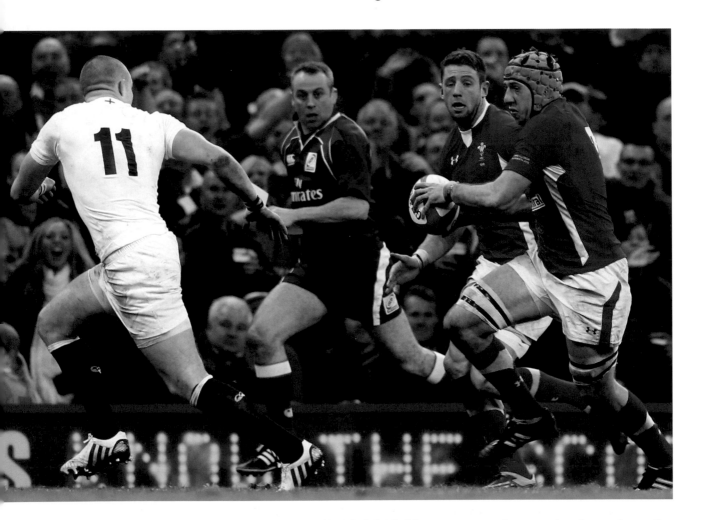

A Six Nations Championship in a British & Irish Lions tour year always seriously cranks up the interest level. Players recognise they are taking part in a series of 'trials' for the tour party, and every armchair critic delivers their predicted squad after each round of the competition. Individual fortunes ebbed and flowed, with the French and Italians happily going about their business, totally oblivious to the background chatter generated by the Lions.

The most obvious effect of the Lions tour was the temporary removal of Warren Gatland from his position as Wales head coach following his appointment as the Lions main man, which focused

attention on every game he attended during the season. It was a constant guessing game about who he could be watching, and the same occurred when his fellow coaches Rob Howley (Wales) and Graham Rowntree and Andy Farrell (both England) finished their commitments with their respective countries.

For Howley, the pressure to defend the Grand Slam title he had helped win for Wales alongside Gatland the previous year was immense and the former scrum half got off to a poor start. A 22-30 home defeat by Ireland – who dominated the first half – suggested the defending champions would struggle to overcome injury problems and the loss of Gatland. How wrong we were!

*ABOVE* Ireland left wing Simon Zebo touches down after ten minutes against Wales at the Millennium Stadium.

*FACING PAGE* Justin Tipuric prepares to send Alex Cuthbert on his way for his second try against England in Cardiff.

The Six Nations coaches attracted plenty of attention, with three of the countries featuring new men in charge: Stuart Lancaster had been installed as England's permanent head coach, Scott Johnson was in charge of Scotland following Andy Robinson's departure, Philippe Saint-André was the latest to try and bring the best out of the French.

The opening weekend of fixtures delivered Wales that home loss thanks to an inspired first-half performance from Ireland and a wonderful piece of individual footballing skill from wing Simon Zebo which suggested they may be a real force in the title race. However, it was to prove their best 40 minutes of rugby in the campaign, while the fightback Wales produced was a portent of things to come. For now, Wales fans had to endure an eighth successive Test defeat and the fact that the Ireland result brought Wales's run of home Test defeats to five, equalling their worst sequence since they started playing international rugby in 1881.

However, the most stunning result of the opening weekend came in the Stadio Olimpico in Rome, where history was made by Italy as they knocked over France for a second time at home (23-18)

amid wild scenes of celebration. It was the second successive time France had lost in Rome, and the defeat tarnished Saint-André's reputation, which had been boosted by victories in the autumn over Australia and Argentina. Leading 15-13 at half-time after rebounding from an early try from Italy captain Sergio Parisse, the French could not find the cohesion to shackle an Italian side that played a more expansive game inspired by their leader.

It overshadowed England's comfortable 38-18 home win over Scotland, who were looking set for another difficult campaign under Johnson, who had added Sky Sports rugby pundit Dean Ryan, the former England No. 8 and Gloucester director of rugby, to his coaching team to take charge of the forwards. Owen Farrell kicked 18 points for England at the start of a great campaign for the youngster, but No. 8 Ben Morgan suffered an ankle injury that would keep him out of the rest of the championship.

The second round of matches proved to be a wake-up call for Italy, who slumped 34-10 to Scotland as Stuart Hogg confirmed his arrival as a full back of outstanding attacking potential with one of four tries. Ryan's forwards stood up well to the Italian challenge, and the Murrayfield crowd went home well satisfied – not something that has happened too often in recent matches.

*ABOVE* Come in No. 36. Billy Twelvetrees, nicknamed '36', powers over the line to score on his England debut, against Scotland at Twickenham.

*RIGHT* Italy skipper Sergio Parisse salutes his side's second successive home win over France in the Six Nations. They would later beat Ireland, too.

For France, the season got even worse with a 16-6 home defeat by Wales, who continued the form they had shown in the second half against Ireland. Big George North, the Wales wing, grabbed a try and was then approached by a pitch invader who wanted to celebrate with him. The man was helped away by stewards still waving his arms in celebration, and it turned out to be George's dad. 'Obviously it's a great story but it's a bit embarrassing for me having my father running on the pitch in a Six Nations match,' said the wing. The game was also notable for the terrible state of the Stade de France pitch, large areas rolling up like a green carpet at every scrum.

There was also good news off the pitch for Wales, who had been hampered by injuries to key players, with flanker Dan Lydiate and lock Alun Wyn Jones predicted to be fit for the potential Slam shoot-out with England.

Ireland's hope that their win in Cardiff was going to signal a season of triumph was abruptly ended by England, who emerged victorious 12-6 at the Aviva Stadium, and while they didn't pull up any trees, at least the win was revenge for the loss they suffered which ruined Grand Slam hopes two years earlier. They dealt with the loss of James Haskell with a yellow card. Farrell kicked two penalties during that period and four overall, with captain Chris Robshaw Man of the Match. It was an award he would warrant in almost every game, yet still found himself surplus to requirements when the British & Irish Lions squad was announced.

Things got even worse for the Irish as they headed to Murrayfield for what appeared to be a game they could win, only to return across the Irish Sea beaten 12-8 by Kelly Brown's combative Scots. Ireland were without banned prop Cian Healy and the injured Jonathan Sexton and Gordon D'Arcy – and they were missed. At Twickenham England knew that despite two early losses, the French would come out with all guns blazing, and a wonderful individual try by Wesley Fofana, exposing defensive weaknesses that would dog England wing Chris Ashton throughout the championship, seemed to

confirm this fact. However, Owen Farrell's incredible kicking was crucial as England remained unbeaten thanks to a 23-13 win that saw recalled centre Manu Tuilagi need 19 stitches to repair a nasty gash to his ear.

Italy, now without the banned Sergio Parisse, who verbally abused a referee during a Top 14 game for Stade Français, could not repeat their French heroics in Rome and they lost 26-9 to a Wales side that was, evidently, going to be a serious hurdle for Grand Slam-chasing England on the final weekend of the tournament.

The penultimate weekend of rugby was notable for a draw which occurred in Dublin, with Ireland and France ending 13-13, which didn't do either side's cause much good and typified the way both teams were operating in the championship. The pressure started to build on Ireland head coach Declan Kidney and he was only too aware that the tricky trip to Rome in the final round of matches was going to have a huge bearing on his future in the job. France only snatched a draw thanks to Freddy Michalak's conversion.

Scotland's early promise did not lead to further momentous days at Murrayfield and it was Wales who claimed a 28-18 win thanks to a Richard Hibbard try and seven penalties and a conversion from Leigh Halfpenny. Scotland lock Richie Gray suffered a terrible hamstring injury and did well to return in time for the Lions tour.

England did not expect to have to take on a Parisse-led Italian side, but his ban was reduced and one of the greatest players to ever appear in the Six Nations bolstered his team's cause at a nervy Twickenham. England stayed on course for the Slam with an 18-11 win that confirmed that while Wales were getting better with every game, the English had peaked earlier in the championship and were now treading water, with players such as Ashton a pale shadow of their former selves. Six Toby Flood penalties constituted the English scoring.

Lancaster had brought in prop Mako Vunipola, hooker Tom Youngs, flanker James Haskell and half backs Flood and Danny Care, but it didn't provide the necessary spark. There was some good news with Tom Croft's return to the match squad after recovering from neck surgery, and the Leicester flanker would force his way into the Lions squad – a remarkable achievement.

Italy rounded off their historic campaign by claiming a first Six Nations victory over Ireland with a 22-15 triumph in their clash at the Stadio Olimpico in Rome on what was supposed to be a celebration of Brian O'Driscoll's last game for his country. It now appears he will be playing on, but this Italian job will not live long in his memory. It also did for coach Declan Kidney, who is no longer in charge of the Ireland team thanks to an almost farcical performance.

O'Driscoll spent ten minutes in the sin-bin for stamping, against an Italian side inspired by skipper Parisse and retiring prop Andrea Lo Cicero. For Lo Cicero, Italy's most-capped player, it was a farewell to remember and enabled the Azzurri to finish the Six Nations with two victories, Irish indiscipline helping matters, with the visitors – at times – reduced to 13 men.

All eyes were now on the Millennium Stadium where the atmosphere was electric as England attempted to win the championship and Wales were determined to stage a party of their own. England went into the game with only a six-day turnaround from the Italy match – and it showed. England's starting XV in Cardiff possessed just 290 caps compared with a Welsh side that had amassed 648, with props Gethin Jenkins and Adam Jones having helped win three Slam titles.

England were blown away 30-3 by an all-consuming surge from Wales. Wing Alex Cuthbert's second-half try double allied to Leigh Halfpenny's four penalties and a Dan Biggar dropped goal, penalty and conversion delivered the heaviest loss of head coach Stuart Lancaster's reign to date.

Wales needed a minimum seven-point win to deny England the title; in the event the winning margin eclipsed the previous best beating of the old enemy, 25-0, 108 years earlier. It was the first time since 1979 that Wales had successfully defended a Five or Six Nations title, and Howley was able to savour a notable triumph – without Gatland at his side. It was a great moment for one of the game's nice guys, and the party in the streets of Cardiff lasted into the early hours.

*FACING PAGE* Scotland have the ball in the safe hands of Jim Hamilton during their 12-8 defeat of Ireland at Murrayfield

*BELOW* Sam Warburton, playing as a foot soldier for the day, charges upfield during Wales's destruction of England in Cardiff.

# The Club Scene
## England: There is Life Below the Elite by NEALE HARVEY

'A fabulous crowd of almost 4000 turned up at Dry Leas, on the banks of the River Thames, to see Henley thrash Worthing in their National Two South title decider in late April'

To the casual observer rugby might appear to start and finish with the elite game. The latest new broadcaster on the block, BT Sport, has spent the summer months pumping its wall-to-wall coverage of the Aviva Premiership; the British & Irish Lions understandably dominated proceedings during June and July; and the game, both at home and abroad, continues to be dogged

by ongoing uncertainty over the future of the Heineken Cup, a competition loved by players and supporters but one that certain money-obsessed administrators seem hell-bent on destroying.

However, one look at Stuart Lancaster's recently announced England Elite Player Squad provides compelling evidence that rugby below elite level is thriving. Of the 65 players named by Lancaster, who learnt his trade in the second tier, around half the squad have experience of playing in the Championship or the leagues below. Joe Launchbury, for example, was once rejected by Harlequins but rebuilt his career at Worthing before hitting the big time with London Wasps.

It is well documented that the admirable Dan Cole cut his teeth at Bedford and Nottingham before cementing a place at Leicester, while the phenomenal transformation of Tom Youngs from bit-part centre to Lions hooker was in no small part due to the two years he spent learning his new position at Nottingham. Owen Farrell spent time at Bedford, Joe Marler at Esher, Freddie Burns at Moseley, Mako Vunipola at Bristol and Billy Twelvetrees at Bedford. All served time in the lower leagues before moving on and there are countless others amongst England's chosen men.

**ABOVE** Newcastle players celebrate their 15-6 win over Leeds in the Championship play-off semi-final second leg. Newcastle went through 34-30 on aggregate.

**LEFT** Bedford's Nick Fenton-Well crashes into Joseph Duffy of Nottingham as the Blues triumph 23-21 at Meadow Lane and 49-38 on aggregate to book their place in the Championship play-off final.

The moral of this tale is that rugby below the elite is booming. If it were not, why are so many Premiership clubs now loaning players to second- and third-tier outfits under the RFU's dual-registration scheme? Exeter Chiefs utility back Jack Nowell is a prime example, having started last season on loan at the Cornish Pirates and ended it as a Premiership regular with Chiefs, a Junior World Championship winner with England Under 20s and an England Saxon to boot.

Ditto the movement of players between the Championship and the Premiership. Last summer, around two dozen players were plucked from obscurity to star in the top flight, with the likes of Gloucester's Rob Cook (ex-Cornish Pirates) and Sione Kalamafoni (Nottingham) being outstanding examples. This summer has seen similar upward movement between the divisions and if you have not yet heard of Josh Bassett (Bedford to Wasps) and Eamonn Sheridan (Rotherham to London Irish), the chances are you will over the coming months and seasons.

There are copious hidden gems out there and the standard of rugby beneath the elite is improving exponentially. The RFU Championship, newly sponsored thanks to the generosity of Greene King IPA, may have been dominated by Newcastle last season, but it produced enough thrills and spills to ensure the Geordies did not always have things their own way. A post-Christmas slump saw them run close by the likes of London Scottish, Nottingham and Bedford before Bristol finally knocked them over on the last day of the regular season, winning 19-14 at Kingston Park.

Newcastle wobbled in the play-offs, too, having to recover from a first-leg deficit before narrowly defeating Leeds in the semi-final and then disposing of Bedford home and away to regain their place in the Premiership at the first time of asking. Led by the reinvigorated Dean Richards, back in the game after serving a three-year ban for his part in the notorious 'Bloodgate' affair at Harlequins, Newcastle will be far stronger for their year in the Championship. Exeter Chiefs proved that coming into the top flight as a battle-hardened outfit can pay dividends down the line.

Leeds enjoyed a strong campaign and may well challenge for promotion this time around, although Bristol will be the favourites after spending big in the wake of Andy Robinson's appointment as director of rugby last February. Robinson's arrival spelt curtains for Liam Middleton, who quickly left the club. The Newcastle victory aside, it was a poor season for Bristol. But not as poor as Doncaster, whose eight-year stay in Level 2 ended in a disappointing first ever relegation.

The Yorkshire outfit return to National League One, from where Ealing Trailfinders emerged after completing a remarkable ascent from the London Leagues to the Championship. Long-serving director of rugby Mike Cudmore deserves all the accolades, having engineered their rise, and they should not be underestimated. Ealing's promotion means no shortage of London derbies in the Championship next season, with London Welsh and London Scottish on the doorstep.

Dropping out of National One were Macclesfield, Sedgley Park and Cambridge, with their places in Level 3 being taken by Henley, Hull Ionians and Worthing. A fabulous crowd of almost 4000 turned up at Dry Leas, on the banks of the River Thames, to see Henley thrash Worthing in their National Two South title decider in late April. But Worthing, under the direction of former London Irish and Ireland flanker Kieron Dawson, staged a remarkable recovery a week later by pulling off a last-gasp play-off victory at Stourbridge to win promotion and reach their highest level ever.

Ampthill, under the guidance of former Newport and Wasps coach Paul Turner, achieved promotion from National Three Midlands, while Bishop's Stortford, Chester and the London Irish Wild Geese clinched the London, North and South West divisions respectively. The Wild Geese are an interesting case in that from next season their ties with Premiership outfit London Irish will be strengthened, with a number of players expected to interchange between the two clubs.

National League clubs no longer participate in cups, but lower league knockout competitions continue to thrive and Brighton RFC took pride of place by defeating Bridlington 30-22 to lift the Intermediate Cup at Twickenham. Selby claimed the Senior Vase and Newent the Junior Vase, while Lancashire defeated Cornwall in thrilling fashion to lift the Bill Beaumont Cup in front of 25,000 at Twickenham, once again proving there is life below the elite. More please!

# next

# Scotland: Glasgow Forge Ahead

## by ALAN LORIMER

'There had been questions about Gregor Townsend's ability to be head coach of Glasgow Warriors. In the event the former Scotland and Lions fly half proved he was the man for the job'

Some decades back, Glasgow's marketing gurus came up with the catchy advertising slogan 'Glasgow's miles better'. It received the cynical response it probably deserved at the time, including a waggish retort from the city's east coast rival which read 'Edinburgh's slightly superior'. Some 30 years later, however, the 1980s slogan, when applied to rugby, now rings true. At the end of a season when the fortunes of Glasgow and Edinburgh could hardly have been more spectrally opposite, Warriors reached the semi-final of the RaboDirect play-offs, only to lose narrowly to the eventual champions, Leinster, in Dublin, but they were still able to reflect on a league campaign that ended with a third-place finish.

There had been questions about Gregor Townsend's ability to be head coach of Glasgow Warriors. In the event the former Scotland and Lions fly half, who had been Andy Robinson's assistant with Scotland, proved he was the man for the job by inspiring his side to a number of spectacular league wins, among them massive victories over Munster and Newport-Gwent Dragons. The solitary blip on his record card was achieving only one win in the Heineken Cup.

Townsend built on the base established by his predecessor, Sean Lineen, and then added his own ideas on attacking rugby and crucially gave a number of younger players their chance to step forward. The Warriors coach also made several shrewd signings, all of whom have been significant factors in both the style and substance of rugby at Scotstoun.

One of these was the Warriors player of the year, Fijian scrum half Niko Matawalu, whose Sevens style of rugby provided the tempo Townsend

**RIGHT** Gregor Townsend with his captain Al Kellock after Glasgow had beaten Edinburgh 44-31 on aggregate to retain the 1872 Cup, contested over the season's two RaboDirect meetings.

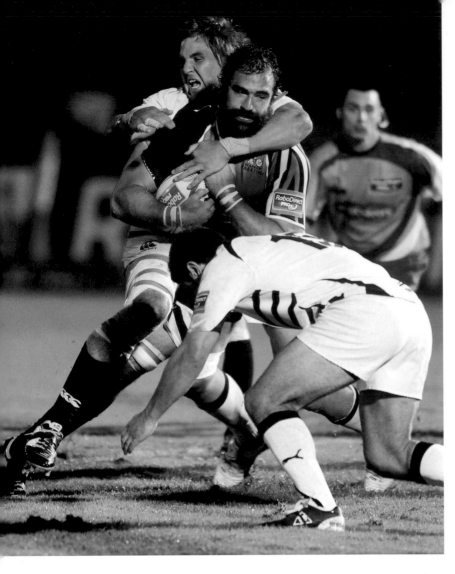

needed for his more expansive game and who rapidly became a cult hero of the Warriors fans. Equally important in the Warriors success were two other Townsend signings, Josh Strauss, an abrasive back-row able to run through defences, and of course the talented Lions wing/full back Sean Maitland.

If Stuart Hogg had been the find of the previous season, then it was the centre/fly half Peter Horne who emerged as the new talent, while in the forwards, hooker Pat MacArthur began to realise his potential. Add to that an existing pool of riches that include the likes of Scotland fly halves Duncan Weir and Ruaridh Jackson, Scotland scrum half Henry Pyrgos (who effectively took over from the injured Chris Cusiter) and Scotland and Lions prop Ryan Grant and it is easy to understand why Townsend was able to shape a winning side.

Glasgow Warriors' new spirit was mirrored by the club's brand new surroundings, the switch from the drab environs of Partick Thistle's stadium at Firhill, which suffered from a narrow pitch, to the attractive and accessible Scotstoun ground in the west of the city proving a 'hit' with both fans and players alike.

Accessible it may be as well, but Murrayfield remains a problem for Edinburgh Rugby. The national stadium, which can be an uplifting cauldron of sound and a cathedral for passionate expression on Six Nations days, becomes a cavernous empty space on league nights, its 67,500 capacity swallowing up the small crowds who support the capital side.

Had the issue of playing in a vastly oversized stadium been Edinburgh's only problem, then professional rugby in the east of Scotland might not have received such negative publicity. The reality is that Edinburgh were beset by many problems both on an off the field.

Matters went awry initially with a number of ill-received signings, part of a spending splurge by Edinburgh and Glasgow to beef up their squads following a loosening of the SRU purse strings. But while Glasgow were judged to have spent wisely, it is generally conceded that Edinburgh brought in players who ultimately contributed little to the cause.

Then there was the playing record, which went from poor to awful, culminating in the forced resignation of head coach Michael Bradley after only 20 months in the job. Bradley had taken Edinburgh to the semi-finals of the Heineken Cup in the previous season, but a whitewash in the 2012-13 competition and a disastrous run in the RaboDirect PRO12 league placed the Irishman in an untenable position.

The febrile atmosphere at Edinburgh also persuaded defence coach Billy McGinty and then forwards adviser Neil Back to depart from Murrayfield. Steve Scott and Duncan Hodge, who had assisted with the national team, were put in charge on an interim basis and the pair at least managed to salvage a little pride from the wreckage.

There were slivers of silver adhering to Edinburgh's rather dark grey cloud, notably the emergence of the young scrum half Sean Kennedy, who had been transferred from Glasgow. The former Stirling player, who had impressed on the IRB Sevens circuit, was rewarded with a Scotland A cap and now looks set to challenge for full international selection.

Just why Edinburgh performed so miserably is hard to fathom. One reason might be that the capital side lacked an experienced fly half. Several young 10s, the pick of which was Harry Leonard, were given a chance, but Bradley never gave any of them a sustained run.

There is a feeling, too, that with only two professional teams, Scottish rugby can ill afford to import foreign players if there is to be room for home-grown talent to develop. Edinburgh perhaps brought in too many non-qualified players, and in an underperforming side they became scapegoats.

Most Scottish rugby fans, however, instantly recognise that the real issue is the lack of a third professional side, which they see as desperately needed if Scotland are to compete internationally. In the absence of a third pro team, the amateur game has steadily sought to reduce the gap between it and the professional overlay, and certainly the ability of amateurs to play at professional level when called up bears testament to raised standards of rugby in this stratum.

Last season Scotland introduced a ten-team Premiership designed to be competitive and to attract the best amateur talent. In the event it was a successful product, providing fans of the game with attractive and hugely competitive rugby from teams that were closely matched.

The exception was Ayr, who set a hot early pace and maintained it to achieve a league and cup double, with Gala taking the runners-up spot in the Premiership and Melrose the consolation prize in the cup. Both Gala and Melrose were involved in British & Irish Cup competition, and while neither of the two Border clubs, nor Stirling nor Dundee, progressed to the knockout stages there were glory days to savour, notably Gala's home win over London Scottish.

At the other end of the Premiership, Boroughmuir were relegated as the last finisher, while Dundee followed after a dramatic play-off with Hawick, whose dramatic 39-38 win ensured promotion back into the Premiership for the famous Border club. While Hawick had to go into a play-off, Glasgow Hawks, as winners of the second-tier Championship, gained automatic promotion, giving west coast amateur rugby kudos to match that of its professional counterpart.

# Wales: Money Remains Tight

## by DAVID STEWART

'The Scarlets under fledgling coach Simon Easterby had a season to be proud of, even if it did not produce silverware. They were the top-placed region in the RaboDirect'

This was the season when the financial chickens really came home to roost. If ever an illustration was needed of how relative poverty has struck the Welsh regions, it was provided with the unseemly saga of the deliciously talented George North being transferred by the Scarlets to Northampton; without his blessing, and – initially at least – without his knowledge. That this young man went on to be one of the very brightest lights on the world stage following his performances for the Lions in Australia only served to underline not only the modesty of the western region's budget, but also the quality of their decision-making.

For too long now, there has been a dysfunctional relationship between the WRU and the four regional teams that emerged from a restructuring of the Welsh domestic game in the 2002-03

season. The new system was put in place by David Moffett in his then role at the head of the WRU's administration. Having resigned a couple of years later, Moffett returned to the southern hemisphere for a period, before re-emerging as a representative of the regions in their battles with the governing body. As teenagers would say, it was not 'a good look'.

Moffett having departed the Welsh scene for a second time, his role was taken by Stuart Gallacher, a former CEO of the Scarlets. The personnel may have changed, but the battleground remains the same – money. Roger Lewis, successor to Moffett at the WRU, deserves significant credit for the repair job he has done to the union's financial situation. However, many complain this has been at the expense – fiscally and playing-wise – of the regions. Examples include the two extra international matches in the November 'window' and at the end of the home season; mutterings abound of the WRU behaving like a fifth region, effectively in competition.

The two adversaries got as far as appointing a Professional Game Rugby Board to deal with areas of dispute, under the chairmanship of Mr Justice Wyn Williams QC, a long-standing member of Tylorstown RFC. As a metaphor for the inability of both sides to make progress towards a much-needed amicable resolution, this jointly constituted body failed to meet even once in full session. This can be tedious stuff; but it is the unavoidable backdrop to the steady decline of Welsh regional rugby.

Choose your own benchmark. Qualification for a quarter-final of the Heineken Cup – once again, no Welsh teams in 2012-13. Retention of top-class players in Wales – as well as North going, Dan Lydiate and Jamie Roberts are Paris-bound; and a notch down, the likes of Tavis Knoyle and Owen Williams are leaving Llanelli for Gloucester and Leicester respectively (God forbid, perhaps as nothing more than squad members).

Turning to results, the Scarlets under fledgling coach Simon Easterby had a season to be proud of, even if it did not produce silverware. They were the top-placed region in the RaboDirect, qualifying for a play-off semi-final in Belfast. Unfortunately they went down 28-17 to Ulster, but it marked encouraging progress, with a number of younger players emerging from academy ranks to establish themselves in the professional game. After a thin period for the production of tight forwards, Danny Wilson (who doubles as forwards coach, alongside his duties with Wales Under 20s) will enjoy working with the likes of tight-head Samson Lee, hookers Kirby Myhill and Emyr Phillips, and loose-head Rhodri Jones; the latter two have already been capped at full international level.

Leading Lions centre Jonathan Davies is still around for another season at least, to accompany the Williams boys – Liam and Scott – in an exciting back five. With Rhys Priestland returning from injury, and top-class Scots open-side John Barclay joining, the guts of a good 1st XV are in place. As always, their prospects of success in league and cup competitions will depend on the avoidance of injury, and the effectiveness of their bench and back-up squad.

On the commercial front, there will be a wish for bigger crowds on a consistent basis at Parc y Scarlets. Their Heineken form last term was poor, with home defeats to Leinster and Clermont Auvergne bookending defeats in the December double-header to Exeter by 30-20 (away) and 22-16 (home). This season's draw threw up Harlequins, Clermont again and Racing

**LEFT** Owen Williams of Cardiff Blues goes past Munster's Duncan Williams to score in the Welsh region's 17-6 RaboDirect win in Cork.

***ABOVE*** Scarlets flanker Josh
Turnbull is hauled down by
opposite number Tommy
O'Donnell as Munster succumb
18-10 at Parc y Scarlets.

***FACING PAGE*** Eli Walker gives the
Toulouse defence the slip as the
Ospreys beat the French side
17-6 in the Heineken Cup. The
wing scored the game's only try.

Métro, which should encourage locals through the turnstiles. It is, however, a heck of a pool to get out of.

Their west Wales neighbours, the Ospreys, had a frustrating time. A strong late run saw them pipped by the Scarlets to fourth position (66 points to 62) in the league. Shorn of some of the big-name overseas recruits from recent seasons, they were ably led by Alun Wyn Jones, whose quality shone through on that wonderful Sydney night in early July. It is remarkable that this region supplied four tight forwards to the Lions party, Ian Evans being the unlucky one not to see the Test activity of Adam Jones, Richard Hibbard and the skipper. Add the open-side talent of Justin Tipuric plus the experience of Ryan Jones and the promise of new Welsh back-row caps James King and Dan Baker, and the Ospreys back line has a wonderful platform to play behind.

Dan Biggar will once again be directing operations with exciting talent both sides of him, in Rhys Webb, Ashley Beck, Andrew Bishop, plus Jonathan Spratt and teenage outside back Dafydd Howells, both of whom went with the Welsh party to Japan. An interesting new face is Canadian wing Jeff Hassler.

Last term's Heineken campaign promised much, but a 15-15 draw at home to old foe Leicester was fatal. Proof of what they can do was a fine 17-6 December triumph over mighty Toulouse at the Liberty Stadium. Northampton, Castres and Leinster make for a tough pool next time, but the other three teams will look at the Ospreys and think the same.

It was a tricky season for the Cardiff Blues. Some results, particularly against Irish provinces, do not make for happy reading, such as a September home defeat to Ulster by 48-19, and a 59-22 hammering from Leinster in Dublin at the end of October, not to mention surrendering to Connaught 26-22 at the Arms Park in February. A notable tick in the win column was by 17-6 over Munster in Cork at the start of January.

Phil Davies had a challenging time in his new director of rugby role. It is common knowledge that cash available for players is not what it was, and after their starring efforts in Australia, Leigh Halfpenny and Sam Warburton became obvious targets for those with much deeper pockets. Optimism comes in the shape of exciting young players such as wing Harry Robinson, fly half Rhys Patchell, centre Owen Williams, and open-side Josh Navidi. All of these were capped on the Welsh tour to Japan, when Bradley Davies was captain.

The return from Toulon of Gethin Jenkins is a plus, especially as the Blues have again drawn his former club – along with Exeter and Glasgow – in the Heineken. That is a pool from which their supporters will hope to qualify. Last season's sole win in the competition came against fellow strugglers Sale Sharks, 26-14, in the last round of games.

The Dragons continued to struggle. A small playing squad, short of experience, meant another lowly finish in the Rabo. Eleventh place on a mere 28 points led to suggestions their status might be downgraded by the WRU to one of 'a development region'. Their board seem to have taken the hint, ensuring that local boy Toby Faletau does not follow Lydiate to the exit, and recruiting the excellent Lyn Jones from London Welsh as director of rugby.

Andrew Coombs was a poster boy last season for what can be achieved by players who come up through the club and regional system by dint of sheer hard work, and Tom Prydie was rehabilitated sufficiently to gain selection again at national level. In addition to Jason Tovey returning from Cardiff, Italian international Kris Burton joins, along with former Edinburgh No. 8 Netani Talei, all adding class.

Former hooker, and Newport legend, Steve Jones joins his namesake in a tracksuit role, specialising in the scrum. They will be seeking an end to some of the uglier results of last season, most obviously a 60-3 hiding to Glasgow at Rodney Parade in February, and a 52-19 mauling against the Ospreys a month later in Swansea. Once again, it is the Amlin Cup for the Dragons. Much more of this may well bring that downgrading threat to the fore.

Which brings us back to money, and the WRU. Central contracts: surely they are the way ahead?

# Eastdil Secured

## is proud to support

# Wooden Spoon Rugby World

EASTDIL
SECURED

# Ireland: Dublin Tops the Pile Again
## by RUAIDHRI O'CONNOR

'The dominance shown by Lansdowne did call into question whether the league should be decided on the table or if the play-offs used in the past should be reintroduced'

For so long the poor relation of the All Ireland League, Dublin is enjoying its golden age in Irish club rugby. Over the first 20 seasons of the competition, just St Mary's in 2000 lifted the division 1 trophy as a host of clubs tried and failed to break the dominance of the likes of Shannon, Garryowen and Cork Constitution.

That total has been quadrupled in three seasons, with Lansdowne the latest side from the capital to finish top of the pile. Although that does not do Mike Ruddock's team justice. They obliterated the

**BELOW** Player of the Season Craig Ronaldson of Lansdowne gets a kick away as Clontarf's Frank Cogan closes in.

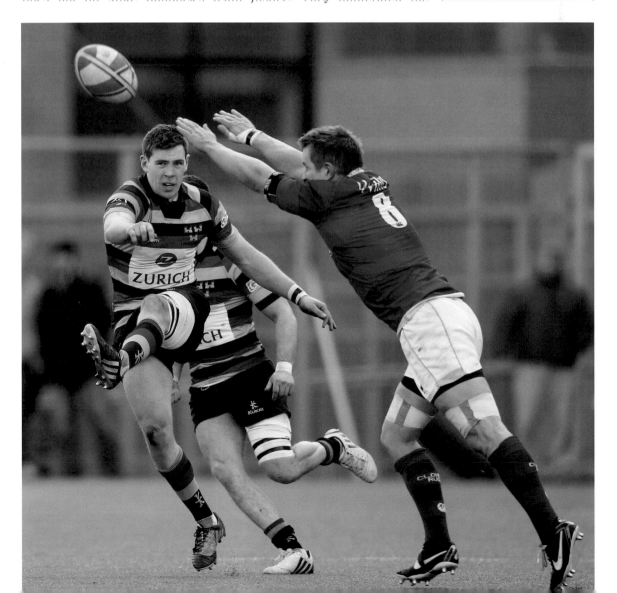

competition to win the title with two games to spare, finishing 18 points clear of Garryowen despite losing both of their last two games after the title had been won. They scored an average of 29 points a game, collecting ten try-scoring bonus points.

Orchestrated by their star out-half and division 1A's Player of the Year Craig Ronaldson (who was also the division's top points scorer), Lansdowne were able to field a mixture of experienced club campaigners and exciting up-and-coming professionals when available. Their back three of captain Ross McCarron, Cian Aherne and Foster Horan caused defences plenty of problems, while their pack led by Willie Earle were a match for any opponent.

They clinched the title on home soil, well turf. The Dubliners play their games under the shadow of the Aviva Stadium on the back pitch, which was upgraded to a 3G synthetic surface after the stadium was redeveloped. With a newly constructed clubhouse and first-class facilities, they were primed to succeed, but the addition of Grand Slam-winning former Wales coach Ruddock completed the jigsaw. Having endured relegation and homelessness during the stadium redevelopment, they clawed their way back to the top flight and then delivered.

For skipper McCarron, who turned his back on a Leinster contract to pursue his career and a life in the amateur game, it was sweet satisfaction, particularly since his father Dermot was club president for the season. 'A few years ago when the stadium was being redeveloped we didn't have a home, didn't have a pitch, but we got two promotions on the bounce under [former coach] Willie Clancy and then Mike and Emmet Farrell came in and we've gone from strength to strength,' he recalled. 'It is amazing, I remember being a ball-boy here, bringing sand on to Eric Elwood taking the kicks. To go from those days to here, to lifting the cup with my Dad as president it is fantastic.'

They got their deliverance with a 32-25 win over second-placed Clontarf on their own pitch on live television. Although their crowning was inevitable with three games to go, they were determined to close the deal on their own pitch and in front of their own home crowd. They did, with Connacht's Ireland Under 20 centre Mark Roche the hero, scoring two tries.

The dominance shown by Lansdowne did call into question whether the league should be decided on the table or if the play-offs used in the past should be reintroduced. Certainly, the best team won and that has not always been the case, but the reward for quality comes at the expense of an end-of-season showpiece and a guaranteed chance of drama to showcase the league.

However, given Lansdowne's form it is likely that they would have won the competition either way, and they followed Old Belvedere and Mary's into the winners' circle, a hat-trick of Dublin clubs after two decades of underachievement. And, as if to emphasise the changing of the guard, Shannon were relegated a week later in humiliating circumstances.

Having battled their way above UL Bohemian and off the bottom spot to earn a promotion/relegation play-off place, they faced UCD at home in Coonagh and the Students produced a performance to remember, running in five tries in a 42-0 win that saw them join Ulster's Ballynahinch in the top flight.

It brought the curtain down on Shannon's glorious 22-year stay in division 1 and 1A, a period that saw them win nine titles and dominate the club game for long stretches. It also saw the end of Marcus Horan's rugby career, the loose-head prop who won the Grand Slam with Ireland during a 67-cap career calling time at the end of the season.

It brought into sharp focus a major issue for the club game: the decline of the provincial sides who have been hit by the poor economy in Ireland. Limerick and Cork have lost players to Dublin, with the capital offering more jobs.

Next season, the Treaty city will have just two clubs – Garryowen and Young Munster – in the top flight, and Shannon chairman Jack Keane commented that there are too many teams competing for too few players in the city. 'I would have said every year for the past ten years, including six years as chairman of Shannon RFC, that there are too many senior clubs in Limerick and Limerick cannot sustain that number,' he said.

'In the past, Limerick has done well on the basis that clubs have been able to find jobs for people, able to get them what they needed. But the whole thing has shifted towards Dublin, I wish Dublin clubs every success.'

At the end of the season, the IRFU published their blueprint for sustainable cubs in an attempt to address some of the issues affecting the club game.

With a number of clubs struggling financially, the union are attempting to stamp out payments to players in order to level the playing field. Only time will tell whether they can be successful.

Outside of the top two divisions, there was reason to celebrate for Terenure College, who won division 2A and promotion to 1B. They will be joined by second-placed Corinthians, with Ballymena and Bruff going the other way.

Rainey Old Boys claimed the division 2B title with 11 points to spare over NUIM Barnhall and both were promoted along with Naas, who overcame Greystones in the play-off. The Wicklow side were relegated from 2A along with Midleton and De La Salle Palmerston. Tullamore and Richmond will replace Clonakilty and Connemara, demoted from 2B, in senior rugby next season.

Cork Constitution claimed the Bateman Cup with a 24-19 win over St Mary's in April, thereby adding the All Ireland Cup trophy to their already laden cabinet in the season the Cork side unveiled their new clubhouse facilities.

Those were officially opened as the club hosted the Ireland Club XV v England Counties match, which the Irish won 30-20 (although they went down 30-18 in Scotland a month later).

It will be remembered as Lansdowne's season and coach Ruddock does not want their dominance to end in 2013.

'When I came in two years ago, I said with the facilities, the location, we have everything going for us, that we should be one of the most potent forces in the league and we have worked hard to do that,' he said.

**BELOW** Templeville Road, Dublin, 27 April 2013. Robert Clune of Cork Constitution scores against St Mary's College in the final of the All Ireland (Bateman) Cup.

'We have put a gym programme in over the summer which has paid a lot of dividends, the boys come in at 7am and train on their nights off. As well as their rugby sessions they train as professionally as they possibly can. The standard in the league has gone up, so we want to have a good standard in our club.'

Whether anyone can match their efforts next year remains to be seen. For now, they can sit back and reflect on their greatest season.

# France: Castres Down Toulon

### by CHRIS THAU

'On the other hand, Castres, with a supporter base of about 50,000, which is the size of the town's population, sits at the centre of the vast rugby-land of Midi-Pyrénées'

**ABOVE** Castres president Michel Dhomps and former president Pierre-Yves Revol parade the Bouclier de Brennus the day after the club's triumph in Paris.

The success of Castres Olympique in the final of the French Championship, arriving as it did several days after their opponents Toulon had lifted the Heineken Cup, the ultimate trophy of European club rugby, was hailed by many in the French game as an act of divine justice. In the eyes of the rugby believer this was David v Goliath, a battle between the small and audacious Castres Olympique, lying tenth in the list of financial muscle in the French league, and the 'Galacticos' of Toulon, a team loaded with international superstars, funded by the second-largest budget in French professional rugby. Furthermore, the relative lack of success of the French national team during the recently concluded season has added a certain piquancy to what was already an increasingly heated debate, about the heart and soul of French rugby and of course its future.

The legendary coach of Stade Toulousain, Guy Novès, observed that his club, a notorious developer of French talent if there has ever been one, had suffered more than most because of the demands of international rugby. While it is heartening to admire the large contingent of Toulouse players gathering for international duty, it is quite clear that the intensity of it and the associated process of wear and tear will take its toll. Consequently, when the Toulouse players rejoin the club after an international weekend, they will need rehabilitation, rest and in some cases medical support, while the performance of the club deteriorates. This is hardly the case with Toulon, with its constellation of international stars.

Furthermore, the head coach of France, Philippe Saint-André, observed that due to an invasion of foreign players French rugby has developed a chronic shortage of international-class performers in key positions, like fly half and scrum half, not to mention prop and hooker. That in turn is altering the fabric of French rugby, with the success-hungry clubs following the Italian/English model of importing talent at an earlier age from South Africa, Fiji, Samoa or Tonga, with the imported players becoming eligible in due course to play for France.

Of course, the reality is a bit more complex, though in fairness the habit of the owner/president of Toulon, Mourad Boudjellal, to make the signing by the club of a world-renowned player a global media circus may have played a part in giving Toulon its mercantile image. The maritime town located at the centre of an urban area with a population ten times that of Castres reigns unchallenged at the top of a financially viable regional rugby edifice, with no major rugby competitor nearby. Its commercial strategy to project itself as a kind of UN of the world of rugby has paid dividends, with the club generating now all the cash it needs to finance its own operations.

On the other hand, Castres, with a supporter base of about 50,000, which is the size of the town's population, sits at the centre of the vast rugby-land of Midi-Pyrénées, competing for support, influence and resources with some of the country's biggest names: the likes of Toulouse, Albi, Béziers, Montauban, Carcassonne and Narbonne. Funding a professional outfit of the size and ambition of Castres Olympique in this environment would have been virtually impossible but for the generosity of the late Pierre Fabre, who was the fifty-fourth-richest man in France and owner of Pierre Fabre Laboratories.

Historically both clubs are among the pioneers of French rugby, supported by dedicated, often compulsive, constituencies. Prior to this final, both had won the French Championship on three occasions: RC Toulonnais in 1931, 1987 and 1992 and Castres Olympique in 1949, 1950 and 1993. However, it is geography and commercial muscle, rather than history, that have defined the public perception of the two clubs and the nature of the argument.

Although Castres have a sizeable community of foreign players in the ranks, the club is nevertheless perceived to be 'more French' than Toulon, whose large contingent of high-profile 'mercenaries' is often attacked as being the symbol of everything that is wrong in French rugby. 'Why is a foreign player labelled "a mercenary" when he signs for Toulon and not for another club?' asked somewhat rhetorically, yet legitimately, Jérôme Lecompte, one of the leaders of the Toulon supporters' association.

*RIGHT* The face of determination. Rory Kockott gets away from Toulon's Jonny Wilkinson to score Castres' try in their 19-14 Top 14 final win at the Stade de France.

This season Castres, coached by Laurent Travers and Laurent Labit, finished the home-and-away phase of the regular season in fourth position with 74 points, while Toulon, under the former France coach Bernard Laporte, topped the table with 90. In the semi-finals Castres despatched Clermont Auvergne 25-9, a clear statement of their potential and ambitions. Meanwhile Toulon knocked out Toulouse, their tormentors in the 2012 final, 24-9 in another act of poetic justice, leaving the former champions with no silverware to show for all their efforts during an arduous and unrewarding season.

The final itself offered glimpses of the one played exactly 20 years earlier, which Castres won against favourites Grenoble, thanks to a dropped goal by the then captain and fly half, the late Francis Rui, which sealed off an unlikely and, to date, controversial win. This time around, with Wilkinson having a modest day with the boot by his standards, it was Castres captain and fly half Rémi Tales who landed two dropped goals in as many minutes to take the match beyond the reach of Toulon, despite their late recovery and a consolation try in injury time.

Somewhat ironically, before the final, the hero of the match, Castres' South African-born scrum half Rory Kockott, who scored an early try and added a further eight points with the boot, had announced his departure for Toulouse. Likewise, the Castres coaching duo Laurent Travers and Laurent Labit have confirmed their departure for Paris, where they will try to add rugby nous and backbone to the so far erratic but well-financed Racing Métro.

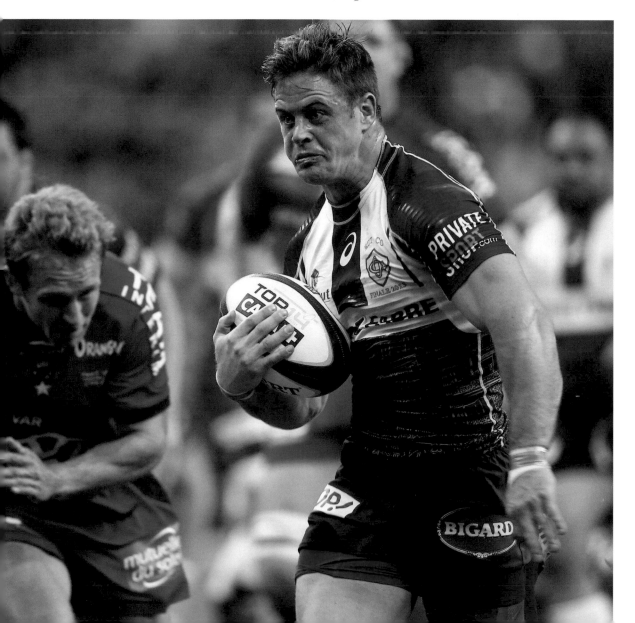

# Italy: Mogliano Take the Prize

## by CHRIS THAU

'Mogliano played well and controlled the game through their savvy scrum half Alberto Lucchese, voted Man of the Match, with right wing Alessandro Onori scoring two tries'

Italian participation in the RaboDirect PRO12 for 2012-13 comprised experienced campaigners Benetton Treviso plus a new outfit, Zebre. Coached by the South African duo Franco Smith and Marius Goosen, with the rugged lock forward Antonio Pavanello as skipper, the former finished the RaboDirect PRO12 league in a notable seventh position, which is not bad at all, taking into account the limitations of their recruitment policy. One must be aware that the selection and promotion of players eligible for Italy is the main priority of Benetton Treviso, as dictated by the Italian Rugby Federation. The same is valid for the Parma-based Zebre – coached last season by Frenchman Christian Gajan and Italians Alex Troncon and Vincenzo Troiani – who finished bottom of the RaboDirect table.

The fact that for the first time ever two Italian players, hooker Leonardo Ghiraldini and flanker Alessandro Zanni, both from Benetton

**BELOW** The Mogliano players with the trophy after beating I Cavalieri Prato 16-11 in the Eccelenza final in Prato.

Treviso, have been selected in the RaboDirect PRO12 Dream Team is not just a coincidence. This is a clear sign of the increased assertiveness of the Italian forwards at both regional and international level.

Altogether, the two Italian professional franchises featured about a dozen non-Italians, mostly of modest pedigree, which is definitely a major handicap against the cash-rich clubs, in particular the English and French. However, in the long term Italian rugby is going to benefit, though coaches, as usual, pay the price for failure. Zebre finished the season without a win from 22 RaboDirect league matches, though they collected nine bonus points, a fact that gives a fair idea about their unfulfilled potential, fully expressed during the last match of the season: a 27-25 defeat at the hands of Munster. The new coach of Zebre is Andrea Cavinato, with Troiani, the only one retained from the previous coaching team, in charge of the forwards.

Furthermore as the use-by date of four senior Italian forwards is approaching, with all four – prop Castrogiovanni, lock forward Bortolami, flanker Mauro Bergamasco and No. 8 and skipper Parisse – having clocked over 90 international caps each, Emerging Italy, nominated last year as the second Italian selection after the Azzurri, gain additional significance in the overall picture of elite development, so far the Achilles' heel of Italian rugby. Within months of his appointment, Italy head coach Jacques Brunel realised that a lack of strength in depth is the chief weakness of Italian rugby, hence his decision to change the name of the second Italian team from Italy A to Emerging Italy. This was definitely not a semantic exercise and the performances of the young Italians against Russia and the Argentina Jaguars and against a bruising Romanian side in the final match of the 2013 IRB Nations Cup tournament prove the point, while giving Brunel hope for the future. The fly-half position has remained one of the main unsolved selectorial issues since the day the little Italo-Argentine maestro Diego Dominguez stepped down as the Azzurri No.10.

Brunel's player of choice for the position has been Luciano Orquera, another Córdoba-born outside half, who spent several unprofitable years with Italy A under the reign of Brunel's predecessors. He made a considerable contribution to Italy's momentous 2013 Six Nations campaign, the win against France in particular, but it is quite clear that the career of the 33-year-old is approaching an end – hence Brunel's decision to give another Italo-Argentine, Alberto di Bernardo of Benetton Treviso, a try during the summer. Di Bernardo made his international debut against South Africa in June, clearly a mountain too high to climb, and his contribution requires further scrutiny before he can match Orquera's deft touches, but there is good news within the ranks of Emerging Italy in the shape of Brisbane-born former Brumbies and Australia Under 20 outside half James Ambrosini, currently playing for Benetton Treviso, and the talented Simone Ragusi of I Cavalieri Prato, who honed his skills with the Ospreys academy two years ago.

To perhaps complement Italy's remarkable Six Nations campaign, in which they beat both France and Ireland, there was an astonishing climax to the Italian domestic league, which saw the underrated Venetian side Marchiol Mogliano, coached by former Italy scrum half Umberto Casellato, defeat I Cavalieri Prato 16-11 to become the eighty-third champions of Italy – the fourteenth club to win the coveted title since it started in 1929. In the semi-finals, Mogliano, fourth at the end of the regular home-and-away championship season, managed to knock out former champions Viadana 24-21 on aggregate. Viadana, who finished at the top of the Italian league table at the end of the 2012-13 season and are coached by former Neath and Wales back-rower Rowland Phillips, had rejoined the top flight of Italian professional club rugby after a break of two years, having benefited from the FIR decision to break up the Aironi professional franchise last year.

The other finalists, I Cavalieri Prato, coached by former Italian No. 8 and captain Andrea de Rossi, knocked out last year's champions Cammi Calvisano 30-20 on aggregate – a very impressive feat indeed. In the final, though, they ran out of steam, with the injury of their Emerging Italy centre Denis Majstorovic in the first minute of the game a significant disrupting factor. Mogliano played well and controlled the game through their savvy scrum half Alberto Lucchese, voted Man of the Match, with right wing Alessandro Onori scoring two tries which made the difference in a tense finale at Prato's Chersoni Stadium. Coach Rossi lost his job at Prato during the summer and was replaced by a former Roma coach, Carlo Pratichetti, while Caselatto left Mogliano for Zebre, where he will be in charge of the backs under new head coach Cavinato. All four semi-finalists have qualified for the 2013-14 Amlin Challenge Cup competition.

# A Summary of the Season 2012-13

### by TERRY COOPER

## INTERNATIONAL RUGBY

### SOUTH AFRICA TO UK & IRELAND, NOVEMBER 2012

| Opponents | Results |
|---|---|
| IRELAND | W 16-12 |
| SCOTLAND | W 21-10 |
| ENGLAND | W 16-15 |
| Played 3 Won 3 | |

### AUSTRALIA TO EUROPE, NOVEMBER/DECEMBER 2012

| Opponents | Results |
|---|---|
| FRANCE | L 6-33 |
| ENGLAND | W 20-14 |
| ITALY | W 22-19 |
| WALES | W 14-12 |
| Played 4 Won 3 Lost 1 | |

### NEW ZEALAND TO EUROPE, NOVEMBER/DECEMBER 2012

| Opponents | Results |
|---|---|
| SCOTLAND | W 51-22 |
| ITALY | W 42-10 |
| WALES | W 33-10 |
| ENGLAND | L 21-38 |
| Played 4 Won 3 Lost 1 | |

### SAMOA TO EUROPE, NOVEMBER 2012

| Opponents | Results |
|---|---|
| WALES | W 26-19 |
| FRANCE | L 14-22 |
| Played 2 Won 1 Lost 1 | |

### TONGA TO EUROPE, NOVEMBER 2012

| Opponents | Results |
|---|---|
| ITALY | L 23-28 |
| SCOTLAND | W 21-15 |
| Played 2 Won 1 Lost 1 | |

### ARGENTINA TO EUROPE, NOVEMBER 2012

| Opponents | Results |
|---|---|
| WALES | W 26-12 |
| FRANCE | L 22-39 |
| IRELAND | L 24-46 |
| Played 3 Won 1 Lost 2 | |

### FIJI TO EUROPE NOVEMBER 2012

| Opponents | Results |
|---|---|
| ENGLAND | L 12-54 |
| Ireland XV | L 0-53 |
| Played 2 Lost 2 | |

### BRITISH & IRISH LIONS TO HONG KONG & AUSTRALIA, JUNE/JULY 2013

| Opponents | Results |
|---|---|
| Barbarians | W 59-8 |
| Western Force | W 69-17 |
| Queensland Reds | W 22-12 |
| Combined Country | W 64-0 |
| NSW Waratahs | W 47-17 |
| Brumbies | L 12-14 |
| AUSTRALIA | W 23-21 |
| Melbourne Rebels | W 35-0 |
| AUSTRALIA | L 15-16 |
| AUSTRALIA | W 41-16 |
| Played: 10 Won 8 Lost 2 | |

### ENGLAND TO ARGENTINA, JUNE 2013

| Opponents | Results |
|---|---|
| ARGENTINA | W 32-3 |
| ARGENTINA | W 51-26 |
| Played 2 Won 2 | |

### WALES TO JAPAN, JUNE 2013

| Opponents | Results |
|---|---|
| JAPAN | W 22-18 |
| JAPAN | L 8-23 |
| Played 2 Won 1 Lost 1 | |

### IRELAND TO USA & CANADA, JUNE 2013

| Opponents | Results |
|---|---|
| USA | W 15-12 |
| CANADA | W 40-14 |
| Played 2 Won 2 | |

## FRANCE TO NEW ZEALAND, JUNE 2013

| Opponents | | Results |
|---|---|---|
| NEW ZEALAND | | L  13-23 |
| NEW ZEALAND | | L  0-30 |
| NEW ZEALAND | | L  9-24 |

Played 3 Lost 3

## CASTLE LAGER INCOMING SERIES

(Held in June in South Africa)

| Samoa | 27 | Scotland | 17 |
|---|---|---|---|
| South Africa | 44 | Italy | 10 |
| Italy | 10 | Samoa | 39 |
| South Africa | 30 | Scotland | 17 |
| Italy | 29 | Scotland | 30 |
| South Africa | 56 | Samoa | 23 |

Champions: South Africa

## ROYAL BANK OF SCOTLAND 6 NATIONS CHAMPIONSHIP 2013

Results

| Wales | 22 | Ireland | 30 |
|---|---|---|---|
| England | 38 | Scotland | 18 |
| Italy | 23 | France | 18 |
| Scotland | 34 | Italy | 10 |
| France | 6 | Wales | 16 |
| Ireland | 6 | England | 12 |
| Italy | 9 | Wales | 26 |
| England | 23 | France | 13 |
| Scotland | 12 | Ireland | 8 |
| Scotland | 18 | Wales | 28 |
| Ireland | 13 | France | 13 |
| England | 18 | Italy | 11 |
| Italy | 22 | Ireland | 15 |
| Wales | 30 | England | 3 |
| France | 23 | Scotland | 16 |

Final Table

| | P | W | D | L | F | A | PD | Pts |
|---|---|---|---|---|---|---|---|---|
| Wales | 5 | 4 | 0 | 1 | 122 | 66 | 56 | 8 |
| England | 5 | 4 | 0 | 1 | 94 | 78 | 16 | 8 |
| Scotland | 5 | 2 | 0 | 3 | 98 | 107 | -9 | 4 |
| Italy | 5 | 2 | 0 | 3 | 75 | 111 | -36 | 4 |
| Ireland | 5 | 1 | 1 | 3 | 72 | 81 | -9 | 3 |
| France | 5 | 1 | 1 | 3 | 73 | 91 | -18 | 3 |

## UNDER 20 SIX NATIONS 2013

Results

| England | 15 | Scotland | 6 |
|---|---|---|---|
| Italy | 6 | France | 13 |
| Wales | 17 | Ireland | 15 |
| Scotland | 30 | Italy | 17 |
| Ireland | 16 | England | 15 |
| France | 13 | Wales | 27 |
| Italy | 10 | Wales | 25 |
| Scotland | 21 | Ireland | 20 |
| England | 40 | France | 10 |
| Scotland | 17 | Wales | 42 |
| Ireland | 22 | France | 5 |
| England | 52 | Italy | 7 |
| Italy | 25 | Ireland | 25 |

| Wales | 15 | England | 28 |
|---|---|---|---|
| France | 13 | Scotland | 10 |

Final Table

| | P | W | D | L | F | A | PD | Pts |
|---|---|---|---|---|---|---|---|---|
| England | 5 | 4 | 0 | 1 | 150 | 54 | 96 | 8 |
| Wales | 5 | 4 | 0 | 1 | 126 | 83 | 43 | 8 |
| Ireland | 5 | 2 | 1 | 2 | 98 | 83 | 15 | 5 |
| Scotland | 5 | 2 | 0 | 3 | 84 | 107 | -23 | 4 |
| France | 5 | 2 | 0 | 3 | 54 | 105 | -51 | 4 |
| Italy | 5 | 0 | 1 | 4 | 65 | 145 | -80 | 1 |

## IRB PACIFIC NATIONS CUP 2013

(Held in May/June)

| Japan | 17 | Tonga | 27 |
|---|---|---|---|
| Canada | 16 | USA | 9 |
| Fiji | 22 | Japan | 8 |
| Fiji | 18 | Canada | 20 |
| Canada | 36 | Tonga | 27 |
| USA | 9 | Tonga | 18 |
| Fiji | 35 | USA | 10 |
| Japan | 16 | Canada | 13 |
| Tonga | 21 | Fiji | 34 |
| Japan | 38 | USA | 20 |

Champions: Fiji

## IRB NATIONS CUP 2013

(Held in June in Bucharest, Romania)

| Romania | 30 | Russia | 20 |
|---|---|---|---|
| Argentina Jaguars | 6 | Emerging Italy | 26 |
| Romania | 30 | Argentina Jaguars | 8 |
| Russia | 19 | Emerging Italy | 27 |
| Argentina Jaguars | 30 | Russia | 17 |
| Romania | 26 | Emerging Italy | 13 |

Champions: Romania
Runners-up: Emerging Italy

## IRB JUNIOR WORLD CHAMPIONSHIP 2013

(Held in June in France)

Semi-finals

| South Africa | 17 | Wales | 18 |
|---|---|---|---|
| New Zealand | 21 | England | 33 |

Third-place Play-off

| South Africa | 41 | New Zealand | 34 |
|---|---|---|---|

Final

| Wales | 15 | England | 23 |
|---|---|---|---|

## IRB JUNIOR WORLD RUGBY TROPHY 2013

(Held in May/June in Chile)

Third-place Play-off

| Chile | 38 | Japan | 35 |
|---|---|---|---|

Final

| Italy | 45 | Canada | 23 |
|---|---|---|---|

## FIRA/AER EUROPEAN UNDER 18 CHAMPIONSHIP 2013 – ELITE DIVISION

(Held in March in France)

*Quarter-finals*

| | | | |
|---|---|---|---|
| England | 82 | Portugal | 8 |
| France | 32 | Italy | 0 |
| Ireland | 31 | Georgia | 27 |
| Scotland | 18 | Wales | 17 |

*Seventh-place Play-off*

| | | | |
|---|---|---|---|
| Portugal | 7 | Italy | 13 |

*Fifth-place Play-off*

| | | | |
|---|---|---|---|
| Wales | 50 | Georgia | 0 |

*Semi-finals*

| | | | |
|---|---|---|---|
| England | 25 | Scotland | 12 |
| France | 23 | Ireland | 18 |

*Third-place Play-off*

| | | | |
|---|---|---|---|
| Ireland | 40 | Scotland | 0 |

*Final*

| | | | |
|---|---|---|---|
| France | 22 | England | 27 |

## THE RUGBY CHAMPIONSHIP 2012

(Formerly the Tri-Nations)

| | | | |
|---|---|---|---|
| Australia | 19 | New Zealand | 27 |
| South Africa | 27 | Argentina | 6 |
| New Zealand | 22 | Australia | 0 |
| Argentina | 16 | South Africa | 16 |
| New Zealand | 21 | Argentina | 5 |
| Australia | 26 | South Africa | 19 |
| New Zealand | 21 | South Africa | 11 |
| Australia | 23 | Argentina | 19 |
| South Africa | 31 | Australia | 8 |
| Argentina | 15 | New Zealand | 54 |
| South Africa | 16 | New Zealand | 32 |
| Argentina | 19 | Australia | 25 |

Champions: New Zealand

## RUGBY WORLD CUP SEVENS 2013

(Held in June in Moscow, Russia)

*Women's Bowl Final*

| | | | |
|---|---|---|---|
| Netherlands | 10 | Fiji | 12 |

*Women's Plate Final*

| | | | |
|---|---|---|---|
| England | 5 | Australia | 14 |

*Women's Third-place Play-off*

| | | | |
|---|---|---|---|
| USA | 10 | Spain | 5 |

*Women's Final*

| | | | |
|---|---|---|---|
| New Zealand | 29 | Canada | 12 |

*Men's Bowl Final*

| | | | |
|---|---|---|---|
| Russia | 29 | Japan | 5 |

*Men's Plate Final*

| | | | |
|---|---|---|---|
| Samoa | 12 | Canada | 19 |

*Men's Third-place Play-off*

| | | | |
|---|---|---|---|
| Fiji | 29 | Kenya | 5 |

*Men's Final*

| | | | |
|---|---|---|---|
| New Zealand | 33 | England | 0 |

## HSBC SEVENS WORLD SERIES FINALS 2012-13

*Australia (Gold Coast)*

| | | | |
|---|---|---|---|
| Fiji | 32 | New Zealand | 14 |

*Dubai*

| | | | |
|---|---|---|---|
| Samoa | 26 | New Zealand | 15 |

*South Africa (Port Elizabeth)*

| | | | |
|---|---|---|---|
| New Zealand | 47 | France | 12 |

*New Zealand (Wellington)*

| | | | |
|---|---|---|---|
| England | 24 | Kenya | 19 |

*USA (Las Vegas)*

| | | | |
|---|---|---|---|
| New Zealand | 21 | South Africa | 40 |

*Hong Kong*

| | | | |
|---|---|---|---|
| Wales | 19 | Fiji | 26 |

*Japan (Tokyo)*

| | | | |
|---|---|---|---|
| New Zealand | 19 | South Africa | 24 |

*Scotland (Glasgow)*

| | | | |
|---|---|---|---|
| South Africa | 28 | New Zealand | 21 |

*England (Twickenham)*

| | | | |
|---|---|---|---|
| New Zealand | 47 | Australia | 12 |

Champions: New Zealand

## WOMEN'S SIX NATIONS 2013

*Results*

| | | | |
|---|---|---|---|
| Italy | 13 | France | 12 |
| England | 76 | Scotland | 0 |
| Wales | 10 | Ireland | 12 |
| France | 32 | Wales | 0 |
| Ireland | 25 | England | 0 |
| Scotland | 0 | Italy | 8 |
| Scotland | 3 | Ireland | 30 |
| England | 20 | France | 30 |
| Italy | 15 | Wales | 16 |
| Ireland | 15 | France | 10 |
| England | 34 | Italy | 0 |
| Scotland | 0 | Wales | 13 |
| France | 76 | Scotland | 0 |
| Italy | 3 | Ireland | 6 |
| Wales | 16 | England | 20 |

*Final Table*

| | P | W | D | L | F | A | PD | Pts |
|---|---|---|---|---|---|---|---|---|
| Ireland | 5 | 5 | 0 | 0 | 88 | 26 | 62 | 10 |
| France | 5 | 3 | 0 | 2 | 160 | 48 | 112 | 6 |
| England | 5 | 3 | 0 | 2 | 150 | 71 | 79 | 6 |
| Wales | 5 | 2 | 0 | 3 | 55 | 79 | -24 | 4 |
| Italy | 5 | 2 | 0 | 3 | 39 | 68 | -29 | 4 |
| Scotland | 5 | 0 | 0 | 5 | 3 | 203 | -200 | 0 |

**FACING PAGE** New Zealand's Pita Anki is wrapped up by John Brake but on a wet day in Moscow New Zealand beat England 33-0 in the final of the Rugby World Cup Sevens.

# CLUB, COUNTY AND DIVISIONAL RUGBY

## ENGLAND

### Aviva Premiership

|  | P | W | D | L | F | A | BP | Pts |
|---|---|---|---|---|---|---|---|---|
| Saracens | 22 | 17 | 1 | 4 | 533 | 339 | 7 | 77 |
| Leicester | 22 | 15 | 1 | 6 | 538 | 345 | 12 | 74 |
| Harlequins | 22 | 15 | 0 | 7 | 560 | 453 | 9 | 69 |
| Northampton | 22 | 14 | 0 | 8 | 501 | 433 | 9 | 65 |
| Gloucester | 22 | 12 | 1 | 9 | 515 | 481 | 10 | 60 |
| Exeter | 22 | 12 | 1 | 9 | 542 | 446 | 9 | 59 |
| Bath | 22 | 10 | 1 | 11 | 452 | 434 | 11 | 53 |
| Wasps | 22 | 9 | 0 | 13 | 511 | 528 | 12 | 48 |
| London Irish | 22 | 7 | 1 | 14 | 459 | 601 | 5 | 35 |
| Sale | 22 | 7 | 1 | 14 | 377 | 596 | 5 | 35 |
| Worcester | 22 | 5 | 1 | 16 | 422 | 547 | 11 | 33 |
| *London Welsh | 22 | 5 | 0 | 17 | 412 | 619 | 8 | 23 |

*Deducted five points for fielding ineligible player*

Relegated: London Welsh

### Aviva Premiership Play-offs

*Semi-finals*

| Leicester | 33 | Harlequins | 16 |
|---|---|---|---|
| Saracens | 13 | Northampton | 27 |

*Final*

| Leicester | 37 | Northampton | 17 |
|---|---|---|---|

### RFU National Championship
Play-Off Winners: Newcastle
Play-Off Runners-up: Bedford

Promoted to Premiership: Newcastle

### National Leagues
National 1 Champions: Ealing Trailfinders
Runners-up: Esher
National 2 (S) Champions: Henley
Runners-up: Worthing
National 2 (N) Champions: Hull Ionians
Runners-up: Stourbridge

National 2 N & S Runners-up Play-off
| Stourbridge | 26 | Worthing | 28 |
|---|---|---|---|

### RFU Knockout Trophy Finals
Intermediate Cup
| Brighton | 30 | Bridlington | 22 |
|---|---|---|---|

Senior Vase
| Selby | 29 | Drybrook | 25 |
|---|---|---|---|

Junior Vase
| Newent | 58 | Baildon | 29 |
|---|---|---|---|

### County Championships
Bill Beaumont Cup Division One Final
| Lancashire | 35 | Cornwall | 26 |
|---|---|---|---|

County Championship Division Two Plate Final
| North Midlands | 10 | Northumberland | 45 |
|---|---|---|---|

County Championship Shield Final
| Cumbria | 16 | Surrey | 21 |
|---|---|---|---|

### National Under 20 Championship Final
| Berkshire | 30 | Cheshire | 17 |
|---|---|---|---|

### National Under 17 Championship Final
| Hornets | 46 | Warrington | 23 |
|---|---|---|---|

### Oxbridge University Matches
Varsity Match
| Oxford | 26 | Cambridge | 19 |
|---|---|---|---|

Under 21 Varsity Match
| Oxford | 31 | Cambridge | 17 |
|---|---|---|---|

Women's Varsity Match
| Oxford | 15 | Cambridge | 5 |
|---|---|---|---|

### BUCS Competitions
Men's Championship Winners: Durham
Women's Championship Winners: Exeter

### Inter-Service Championship
| Royal Air Force | 26 | Royal Navy | 55 |
|---|---|---|---|
| Army | 33 | Royal Air Force | 18 |
| Army | 43 | Royal Navy | 26 |

Champions: Army

### Hospitals Cup Winners: Barts and The London

### Rosslyn Park Schools Sevens
Open Winners: Sedbergh
Festival Winners: Wellington College
Colts Winners: Competition Cancelled
Preparatory Winners: Aysgarth
Juniors Winners: QEGS Wakefield
Girls Winners: Hartpury College

### Daily Mail RBS Schools Day
Under 18 Cup Winners: Dulwich College
Under 18 Vase Winners: Yarm
Under 15 Cup Winners: Warwick
Under 15 Vase Winners: Royal Latin

### Women's Premiership

|  | P | W | D | L | PF | PA | BP | Pts |
|---|---|---|---|---|---|---|---|---|
| Worcester | 14 | 12 | 0 | 2 | 534 | 142 | 10 | 58 |
| Richmond | 14 | 12 | 1 | 1 | 435 | 153 | 7 | 57 |
| Lichfield | 14 | 10 | 0 | 4 | 422 | 208 | 9 | 49 |
| Bristol | 14 | 8 | 0 | 6 | 313 | 206 | 7 | 39 |
| Wasps | 14 | 5 | 1 | 8 | 236 | 337 | 6 | 28 |
| Saracens | 14 | 5 | 1 | 8 | 213 | 347 | 4 | 26 |
| Darlington MP | 14 | 2 | 0 | 12 | 190 | 483 | 2 | 10 |
| Thurrock | 14 | 0 | 1 | 13 | 102 | 569 | 3 | 5 |

Champions: Worcester

## SCOTLAND

### RBS Cup
*Semi-finals*

| | | | |
|---|---|---|---|
| Gala | 29 | Melrose | 34 |
| Dundee HSFP | 5 | Ayr | 15 |

*Final*

| | | | |
|---|---|---|---|
| Melrose | 25 | Ayr | 28 |

### RBS Shield Final

| | | | |
|---|---|---|---|
| Marr | 30 | Livingston | 15 |

### RBS Bowl Final

| | | | |
|---|---|---|---|
| Grangemouth Stags | 14 | Oban Lorne | 19 |

### Scottish Sevens Winners
Gala: Gala
Melrose: Saracens
Hawick: Hawick
Berwick: Watsonians
Langholm: Selkirk
Peebles: Melrose
Kelso: Watsonians
Earlston: Melrose
Selkirk: Selkirk
Jed-Forest: Jed-Forest
*Kings of the Sevens:* Melrose

### RBS Premiership

| | P | W | D | L | F | A | BP | Pts |
|---|---|---|---|---|---|---|---|---|
| Ayr | 18 | 16 | 0 | 2 | 480 | 317 | 8 | 72 |
| Gala | 18 | 15 | 0 | 3 | 487 | 323 | 9 | 69 |
| Stirling County | 18 | 8 | 1 | 9 | 468 | 529 | 12 | 46 |
| Edinburgh Accies | 18 | 8 | 1 | 9 | 386 | 380 | 10 | 44 |
| Aberdeen GS | 18 | 7 | 1 | 10 | 468 | 485 | 13 | 43 |
| Melrose | 18 | 8 | 0 | 10 | 389 | 422 | 11 | 43 |
| Heriot's | 18 | 7 | 1 | 10 | 434 | 440 | 12 | 42 |
| Currie | 18 | 7 | 3 | 8 | 412 | 465 | 6 | 40 |
| Dundee HSFP | 18 | 7 | 0 | 11 | 453 | 509 | 10 | 38 |
| Boroughmuir | 18 | 3 | 1 | 14 | 350 | 457 | 10 | 24 |

### RBS Premiership Play-off

| | | | |
|---|---|---|---|
| Dundee HSFP | 38 | Hawick | 39 |

### RBS National League

| | P | W | D | L | F | A | BP | Pts |
|---|---|---|---|---|---|---|---|---|
| Glasgow Hawks | 18 | 14 | 1 | 3 | 548 | 246 | 14 | 72 |
| Hawick | 18 | 14 | 2 | 2 | 608 | 366 | 12 | 72 |
| Watsonians | 18 | 10 | 0 | 8 | 497 | 367 | 10 | 50 |
| Selkirk | 18 | 11 | 0 | 7 | 348 | 394 | 6 | 50 |
| Hillhead/J'hill | 18 | 8 | 0 | 10 | 384 | 386 | 10 | 42 |
| Stewart's Melville | 18 | 7 | 2 | 9 | 412 | 463 | 8 | 40 |
| Kelso | 18 | 6 | 0 | 12 | 368 | 421 | 12 | 36 |
| Biggar | 18 | 6 | 2 | 10 | 341 | 440 | 7 | 35 |
| Hamilton | 18 | 6 | 1 | 11 | 422 | 560 | 6 | 32 |
| Jed-Forest | 18 | 4 | 0 | 14 | 287 | 572 | 7 | 23 |

### RBS Women's Premier 1
Champions: Hillhead/Jordanhill

### RBS Women's Premier 2
Champions: Stirling County

## WALES

### SWALEC Cup
*Semi-finals*

| | | | |
|---|---|---|---|
| Carmarthen | 16 | Pontypridd | 18 |
| Aberavon | 22 | Neath | 27 |

*Final*

| | | | |
|---|---|---|---|
| Pontypridd | 34 | Neath | 13 |

### SWALEC Plate Final

| | | | |
|---|---|---|---|
| Heol y Cyw | 20 | Rhydyfelin | 19 |

### SWALEC Bowl Final

| | | | |
|---|---|---|---|
| Fishguard & Goodwick | 17 | Wattstown | 27 |

### Principality Premiership

| | P | W | D | L | F | A | BP | Pts |
|---|---|---|---|---|---|---|---|---|
| Pontypridd | 22 | 21 | 0 | 1 | 715 | 342 | 12 | 96 |
| Llandovery | 22 | 13 | 3 | 6 | 586 | 393 | 15 | 73 |
| Llanelli | 22 | 14 | 0 | 8 | 588 | 407 | 11 | 67 |
| Redwas | 22 | 13 | 1 | 8 | 594 | 505 | 13 | 67 |
| Cross Keys | 22 | 13 | 0 | 9 | 543 | 403 | 14 | 66 |
| Carmarthen | 22 | 11 | 0 | 11 | 476 | 479 | 12 | 56 |
| Newport | 22 | 8 | 2 | 12 | 466 | 588 | 9 | 45 |
| Cardiff Rugby | 22 | 8 | 2 | 12 | 477 | 505 | 8 | 44 |
| Aberavon | 22 | 8 | 1 | 13 | 404 | 535 | 8 | 42 |
| Neath | 22 | 8 | 1 | 13 | 347 | 558 | 6 | 40 |
| Bridgend | 22 | 7 | 0 | 15 | 404 | 573 | 7 | 35 |
| Swansea | 22 | 3 | 0 | 19 | 337 | 649 | 7 | 19 |

### SWALEC Championship

| | P | W | D | L | F | A | BP | Pts |
|---|---|---|---|---|---|---|---|---|
| Ebbw Vale | 26 | 25 | 0 | 1 | 1132 | 280 | 23 | 123 |
| Bargoed | 26 | 20 | 1 | 5 | 715 | 400 | 16 | 98 |
| Cardiff Met | 26 | 17 | 1 | 8 | 619 | 468 | 14 | 84 |
| Tata Steel | 26 | 17 | 1 | 8 | 737 | 496 | 13 | 83 |
| Newbridge | 26 | 15 | 1 | 10 | 573 | 551 | 9 | 71 |
| Narberth | 26 | 14 | 0 | 12 | 608 | 625 | 13 | 69 |
| Llanharan | 26 | 12 | 0 | 14 | 539 | 645 | 17 | 65 |
| Blackwood | 26 | 12 | 0 | 14 | 562 | 688 | 13 | 61 |
| Bridgend Ath. | 26 | 12 | 0 | 14 | 548 | 662 | 12 | 60 |
| Beddau | 26 | 10 | 1 | 15 | 536 | 523 | 15 | 57 |
| Bonymaen | 26 | 9 | 0 | 17 | 399 | 593 | 11 | 47 |
| Pontypool | 26 | 7 | 0 | 19 | 411 | 714 | 8 | 36 |
| The Wanderers | 26 | 4 | 2 | 20 | 437 | 807 | 9 | 29 |
| Whitland | 26 | 4 | 1 | 21 | 388 | 752 | 9 | 27 |

### SWALEC Leagues
Division 1 East Champions: RGC 1404
Division 1 East Runners-up: Ystrad Rhondda
Division 1 North Champions: Nant Conwy
Division 1 North Runners-up: Pwllheli
Division 1 West Champions: Tondu
Division 1 West Runners-up: Cwnllynfell
Division 2 East Champions: Bedlinog
Division 2 East Runners-up: Nelson
Division 2 North Champions: Denbigh
Division 2 North Runners-up: COBRA
Division 2 West Champions: Builth Wells
Division 2 West Runners-up: Crymych

## IRELAND

### Ulster Bank League Division 1A

| | P | W | D | L | F | A | BP | Pts |
|---|---|---|---|---|---|---|---|---|
| Lansdowne | 18 | 14 | 0 | 4 | 524 | 292 | 12 | 68 |
| Garryowen | 18 | 11 | 0 | 7 | 338 | 269 | 6 | 50 |
| Clontarf | 18 | 9 | 0 | 9 | 413 | 315 | 13 | 49 |
| Cork Const'n | 18 | 11 | 0 | 7 | 349 | 435 | 3 | 47 |
| Dolphin | 18 | 8 | 0 | 10 | 366 | 349 | 10 | 42 |
| Young Munster | 18 | 8 | 0 | 10 | 294 | 302 | 8 | 40 |
| Old Belvedere | 18 | 7 | 0 | 11 | 379 | 392 | 12 | 40 |
| St. Mary's Coll. | 18 | 9 | 0 | 9 | 316 | 345 | 3 | 39 |
| Shannon | 18 | 6 | 0 | 12 | 302 | 429 | 7 | 31 |
| UL Bohemian | 18 | 7 | 0 | 11 | 241 | 394 | 3 | 31 |

### Ulster Bank League Division 1B

| | P | W | D | L | F | A | BP | Pts |
|---|---|---|---|---|---|---|---|---|
| Ballynahinch | 18 | 16 | 1 | 1 | 623 | 231 | 9 | 75 |
| UCD | 18 | 14 | 0 | 4 | 556 | 278 | 12 | 68 |
| Dublin University | 18 | 13 | 0 | 5 | 450 | 290 | 10 | 62 |
| Buccaneers | 18 | 10 | 1 | 7 | 387 | 395 | 7 | 49 |
| Malone | 18 | 7 | 1 | 10 | 392 | 414 | 8 | 38 |
| Belfast H'quins | 18 | 7 | 1 | 10 | 350 | 386 | 8 | 38 |
| Blackrock Coll. | 18 | 7 | 2 | 9 | 357 | 410 | 6 | 38 |
| Dungannon | 18 | 6 | 1 | 11 | 385 | 414 | 7 | 33 |
| Ballymena | 18 | 3 | 1 | 14 | 201 | 546 | 5 | 19 |
| Bruff | 18 | 3 | 0 | 15 | 210 | 547 | 6 | 18 |

### Ulster Bank League Division 2A
Champions: Terenure College

### Ulster Bank League Division 2B
Champions: Rainey OB

### Round Robin
| Portadown | 5 | Tullamore | 18 |
|---|---|---|---|
| Richmond | 29 | Monivea | 0 |
| Monivea | 10 | Portadown | 29 |
| Tullamore | 33 | Richmond | 22 |
| Monivea | 17 | Tullamore | 26 |
| Portadown | 5 | Richmond | 15 |

Winners: Tullamore

### All Ireland Cup Final
| St Mary's College | 19 | Cork Constitution | 24 |
|---|---|---|---|

### All Ireland Junior Cup Final
| Enniscorthy | 10 | Tullamore | 29 |
|---|---|---|---|

### Fraser McMullen Under 21 Cup Final
| Lansdowne | 27 | Dublin University | 26 |
|---|---|---|---|

## RABODIRECT PRO12 2012-13

| | P | W | D | L | F | A | BP | Pts |
|---|---|---|---|---|---|---|---|---|
| Ulster | 22 | 17 | 1 | 4 | 577 | 348 | 11 | 81 |
| Leinster | 22 | 17 | 0 | 5 | 585 | 386 | 10 | 78 |
| Warriors | 22 | 16 | 0 | 6 | 541 | 324 | 12 | 76 |
| Scarlets | 22 | 15 | 0 | 7 | 436 | 406 | 6 | 66 |
| Ospreys | 22 | 14 | 1 | 7 | 471 | 342 | 4 | 62 |
| Munster | 22 | 11 | 1 | 10 | 442 | 389 | 8 | 54 |
| Treviso | 22 | 10 | 2 | 10 | 414 | 450 | 6 | 50 |
| Connacht | 22 | 8 | 1 | 13 | 358 | 422 | 4 | 38 |
| Blues | 22 | 8 | 0 | 14 | 348 | 487 | 6 | 38 |
| Edinburgh | 22 | 7 | 0 | 15 | 399 | 504 | 8 | 36 |
| Dragons | 22 | 6 | 0 | 16 | 358 | 589 | 4 | 28 |
| Zebre | 22 | 0 | 0 | 22 | 291 | 573 | 10 | 10 |

### RaboDirect PRO12 Play-offs
*Semi-finals*
| Ulster | 28 | Scarlets | 17 |
|---|---|---|---|
| Leinster | 17 | Warriors | 15 |

*Final*
| Ulster | 18 | Leinster | 24 |
|---|---|---|---|

## LV= CUP 2012-13

*Semi-finals*
| Harlequins | 31 | Bath | 23 |
|---|---|---|---|
| Sale | 21 | Saracens | 15 |

*Final*
| Sale | 14 | Harlequins | 32 |
|---|---|---|---|

## BRITISH & IRISH CUP 2012-13

*Final*
| Newcastle | 17 | Leinster A | 18 |
|---|---|---|---|

## FRANCE

### 'Top 14' Play-offs

*Semi-finals*
| Toulon | 24 | Toulouse | 9 |
|---|---|---|---|
| Clermont Auvergne | 9 | Castres | 25 |

*Final*
| Toulon | 14 | Castres | 19 |
|---|---|---|---|

## ITALY

**Campionato d'Eccellenza**

*Final*
Estra I Cavalieri Prato 11　Marchiol Mogliano　16

## HEINEKEN CUP 2012-13

*Quarter-finals*
| | | | |
|---|---|---|---|
| Clermont Auvergne | 36 | Montpellier | 14 |
| Saracens | 27 | Ulster | 16 |
| Harlequins | 12 | Munster | 18 |
| Toulon | 21 | Leicester | 15 |

*Semi-finals*
| | | | |
|---|---|---|---|
| Clermont Auvergne | 16 | Munster | 10 |
| Saracens | 12 | Toulon | 24 |

*Final*
| | | | |
|---|---|---|---|
| Clermont Auvergne | 15 | Toulon | 16 |

## AMLIN CHALLENGE CUP 2012-13

*Quarter-finals*
| | | | |
|---|---|---|---|
| Gloucester | 31 | Biarritz | 41 |
| Wasps | 28 | Leinster | 48 |
| Perpignan | 30 | Toulouse | 19 |
| Bath | 20 | Stade Français | 36 |

*Semi-finals*
| | | | |
|---|---|---|---|
| Perpignan | 22 | Stade Français | 25 |
| Leinster | 44 | Biarritz | 16 |

*Final*
| | | | |
|---|---|---|---|
| Leinster | 34 | Stade Français | 13 |

## NEW ZEALAND

**ITM Cup Premiership Final 2012**

| | | | |
|---|---|---|---|
| Canterbury | 31 | Auckland | 18 |

**ITM Cup Championship Final 2012**

| | | | |
|---|---|---|---|
| Counties Manukau | 41 | Otago | 16 |

**Heartland Champions 2012**
Meads Cup: East Coast
Lochore Cup: Buller

**Ranfurly Shield holders:** Waikato

## SOUTH AFRICA

**Currie Cup 2012**

*Final*
Sharks　　　18　Western Province 25

## SUPER RUGBY 2013

*Final Table*

| | P | W | D | L | F | A | BP | Pts |
|---|---|---|---|---|---|---|---|---|
| **Chiefs** | **16** | **12** | **0** | **4** | **458** | **364** | **10** | **66** |
| **Bulls** | **16** | **12** | **0** | **4** | **448** | **330** | **7** | **63** |
| **Brumbies** | **16** | **10** | **2** | **4** | **430** | **295** | **8** | **60** |
| *Crusaders* | *16* | *11* | *0* | *5* | *446* | *307* | *8* | *60* |
| *Reds* | *16* | *10* | *2* | *4* | *321* | *296* | *6* | *58* |
| *Cheetahs* | *16* | *10* | *0* | *6* | *382* | *358* | *6* | *54* |
| Stormers | 16 | 9 | 0 | 7 | 346 | 292 | 6 | 50 |
| Sharks | 16 | 8 | 0 | 8 | 384 | 308 | 8 | 48 |
| Waratahs | 16 | 8 | 0 | 8 | 411 | 371 | 5 | 45 |
| Blues | 16 | 6 | 0 | 10 | 347 | 364 | 12 | 44 |
| Hurricanes | 16 | 6 | 0 | 10 | 300 | 457 | 10 | 42 |
| Rebels | 16 | 5 | 0 | 11 | 382 | 515 | 8 | 36 |
| Western Force | 16 | 4 | 1 | 11 | 267 | 366 | 5 | 31 |
| Highlanders | 16 | 3 | 0 | 13 | 374 | 496 | 9 | 29 |
| Southern Kings | 16 | 3 | 1 | 12 | 298 | 564 | 2 | 24 |

*Qualifying finals*
| | | | |
|---|---|---|---|
| Crusaders | 38 | Reds | 9 |
| Brumbies | 15 | Cheetahs | 13 |

*Semi-finals*
| | | | |
|---|---|---|---|
| Chiefs | 20 | Crusaders | 19 |
| Bulls | 23 | Brumbies | 26 |

*Final*
| | | | |
|---|---|---|---|
| Chiefs | 27 | Brumbies | 22 |

Key
**Chiefs**: Conference leaders
*Crusaders*: Wild Card teams

Note: The top two Conference leaders – Chiefs and Bulls – received a bye to the semi-finals

## BARBARIANS

| Opponents | Results |
|---|---|
| ENGLAND | L 12-40 |
| BRITISH & IRISH LIONS | L 8-59 |

Played 2 Lost 2

# PREVIEW OF THE SEASON 2013-14

# Key Players

## selected by IAN ROBERTSON

### ENGLAND

**BILLY TWELVETREES**
Gloucester
Born: 15 November 1988
Height: 6ft 3ins Weight: 15st 10lbs
Centre – 5 caps
1st cap v Scotland 2013

**ALEX CORBISIERO**
Northampton Saints
Born: 30 August 1988
Height: 6ft 1in Weight: 18st 8lbs
Prop – 18 caps (+2 Lions)
1st cap v Italy 2011

### SCOTLAND

**STUART HOGG**
Glasgow Warriors
Born: 24 June 1992
Height: 5ft 11ins Weight: 13st 1lb
Full back – 15 caps
1st cap v Wales 2012

**RYAN GRANT**
Glasgow Warriors
Born: 8 October 1985
Height: 6ft Weight: 17st 2lbs
Prop – 10 caps
1st cap v Australia 2012

### WALES

**JONATHAN DAVIES**
Scarlets
Born: 5 April 1988
Height: 6ft 1in Weight: 16st 5lbs
Centre – 36 caps (+3 Lions)
1st cap v Canada 2009

**TOBY FALETAU**
Dragons
Born: 12 November 1990
Height: 6ft 2ins Weight: 17st 4lbs
Back-row – 26 caps (+1 Lions)
1st cap v Barbarians 2011

# Six Nations Championship

## 2013-14

### IRELAND

**SIMON ZEBO**
Munster
Born: 16 March 1990
Height: 6ft 2ins Weight: 14st 10lbs
Wing – 6 caps
1st cap v New Zealand 2012

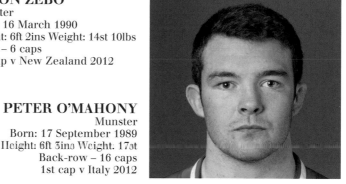

**PETER O'MAHONY**
Munster
Born: 17 September 1989
Height: 6ft 3ins Weight: 17st
Back-row – 16 caps
1st cap v Italy 2012

### FRANCE

**WESLEY FOFANA**
Clermont Auvergne
Born: 20 January 1988
Height: 5ft 10ins Weight: 14st
Centre – 18 caps
1st cap v Italy 2012

**YANNICK NYANGA**
Toulouse
Born: 19 December 1983
Height: 6ft 2ins Weight: 16st
Back-row – 33 caps
1st cap v USA 2004

### ITALY

**ANDREA MASI**
Wasps
Born: 30 March 1981
Height: 6ft Weight: 15st 8lbs
Centre – 80 caps
1st cap v Spain 1999

**LORENZO CITTADINI**
Benetton Treviso
Born: 17 December 1982
Height: 6ft 3ins Weight: 19st 7lbs
Prop – 24 caps
1st cap v Ireland 2008

# Fixtures 2013-14

## AUGUST 2013
Sat. 17th    AUSTRALIA v NZ (RC)
   SA v ARGENTINA (RC)
Sat. 17th and
Sun. 18th    World Club 7s (Twickenham)
Sat. 24th    NZ v AUSTRALIA (RC)
   ARGENTINA v SA (RC)
   RBS Scottish Premiership
   RBS Scottish National Leagues
   RBS Scottish Ch/ship A & B
Sat. 31st    RBS Scottish Premiership
   RBS Scottish National Leagues
   RBS Scottish Ch/ship A & B

## SEPTEMBER 2013
Fri. 6th to
Sun. 8th    Aviva English Premiership (1)
   RaboDirect PRO12 (1)
Sat. 7th    AUSTRALIA v SA (RC)
   NZ v ARGENTINA (RC)
   English National Leagues
   RBS Scottish Premiership
   RBS Scottish National Leagues
   RBS Scottish Ch/ship A & B
   Swalec Welsh Nat Ch/ship
   Swalec Welsh Nat Leagues
Fri. 13th to
Sun. 15th    Aviva English Premiership (2)
   RaboDirect PRO12 (2)
Sat. 14th    AUSTRALIA v ARGENTINA (RC)
   NZ v SA (RC)
   English National Leagues
   RBS Scottish Premiership
   RBS Scottish National Leagues
   RBS Scottish Ch/ship A & B
   Welsh Principality Premiership
   Swalec Welsh Nat Ch/ship
   Swalec Welsh Nat Leagues
Sat. 14th and
Sun. 15th    Greene King IPA Championship
Wed. 18th    Welsh Principality Premiership
Fri. 20th
to Sun. 22nd    Aviva English Premiership (3)
   RaboDirect PRO12 (3)
   Greene King IPA Championship
Sat. 21st    English National Leagues
   RBS Scottish Premiership
   RBS Scottish National Leagues
   RBS Scottish Ch/ship A & B
   Welsh Principality Premiership
   Swalec Welsh Nat Ch/ship
   Swalec Welsh Nat Leagues
Fri. 27th and
Sat 28th    UB Irish Leagues 1A&B & 2B
Fri. 27th to
Sun. 29th    Aviva English Premiership (4)
   RaboDirect PRO12 (4)

Sat. 28th    SA v AUSTRALIA (RC)
   ARGENTINA v NZ (RC)
   Greene King IPA Championship
   English National Leagues
   RBS Scottish Premiership
   RBS Scottish National Leagues
   RBS Scottish Ch/ship A & B
   Welsh Principality Premiership
   Swalec Welsh Nat Ch/ship
   Swalec Welsh Nat Leagues

## OCTOBER 2013
Fri. 4th and
Sat. 5th    SA v NZ (RC)
   ARGENTINA v AUSTRALIA (RC)
   English National Leagues
   RBS Scottish Premiership
   RBS Scottish National Leagues
   RBS Scottish Ch/ship A & B
   Welsh Principality Premiership
   Swalec Welsh Nat Ch/ship
   Swalec Bowl (1)
   UB Irish Lges 1A&B & 2A&B
Fri. 4th to
Sun. 6th    Aviva English Premiership (5)
   RaboDirect PRO12 (5)
   Greene King IPA Championship
   UB Irish Leagues 1A&B & 2B
Thu. 10th to
Sun. 13th    Heineken Cup (1)
   Amlin Challenge Cup (1)
Sat. 12th    English National Leagues
   RBS Scottish Premiership
   RBS Scottish National Leagues
   RBS Scottish Ch/ship A & B
   Swalec Welsh Nat Ch/ship
   Swalec Welsh Nat Leagues
Sat. 12th and
Sun.13th    British & Irish Cup (1)
Thu. 17th to
Sun. 20th    Heineken Cup (2)
   Amlin Challenge Cup (2)
Sat. 19th    NZ v AUSTRALIA
   English National Leagues
   RFU Cup competitions (1)
   RBS Scottish Premiership
   RBS Scottish National Leagues
   RBS Scottish Ch/ship A & B
   Swalec Welsh Nat Ch/ship
   Swalec Welsh Nat Leagues
Sat. 19th and
Sun. 20th    British & Irish Cup (2)
Fri. 25th and
Sat. 26th    UB Irish Leagues 1A&B & 2B
Fri. 25th to
Sun. 27th    Aviva English Premiership (6)
   RaboDirect PRO12 (6)

| | |
|---|---|
| Sat. 26th | Greene King IPA Championship |
| | English National Leagues |
| | RBS Scottish Premiership |
| | RBS Scottish National Leagues |
| | RBS Scottish Ch/ship A & B |
| | Welsh Principality Premiership |
| | Swalec Welsh Nat Ch/ship |
| | Swalec Plate (1) |
| | Swalec Bowl (2) |
| Wed. 30th | Welsh Principality Premiership |

**NOVEMBER 2013**

| | |
|---|---|
| Fri. 1st and Sat. 2nd | UB Irish Leagues 1A&B & 2B |
| Fri. 1st to Sun. 3rd | Aviva English Premiership (7) |
| | RaboDirect PRO12 (7) |
| | Greene King IPA Championship |
| Sat. 2nd | ENGLAND v AUSTRALIA |
| | English National Leagues |
| | RBS Scottish Premiership |
| | RBS Scottish National Leagues |
| | RBS Scottish Ch/ship A & B |
| | Welsh Principality Premiership |
| | Swalec Welsh Nat Ch/ship |
| | Swalec Welsh Nat Leagues |
| Fri. 8th and Sat. 9th | LV= (Anglo-Welsh) Cup (1) |
| Fri. 8th to Sun. 10th | Greene King IPA Championship |
| | UB Irish Leagues 1A&B |
| Sat. 9th | ENGLAND v ARGENTINA |
| | IRELAND v SAMOA |
| | FRANCE v NZ |
| | WALES v SA |
| | SCOTLAND v JAPAN |
| | English National Leagues |
| | RBS Scottish Premiership |
| Fri. 15th to Sun. 17th | Greene King IPA Championship |
| Sat. 16th | FRANCE v TONGA |
| | WALES v ARGENTINA |
| | ENGLAND v NZ |
| | IRELAND v AUSTRALIA |
| | English Nat Leagues 1 & 2 |
| | RFU Cup competitions (2) |
| | RBS Scottish Premiership |
| | RBS Scottish National Leagues |
| | RBS Scottish Ch/ship A & B |
| Sat. 16th and Sun. 17th | LV= (Anglo-Welsh) Cup (2) |
| Sun. 17th | SCOTLAND v SA |
| Fri. 22nd | WALES v TONGA |
| Fri. 22nd and Sat. 23rd | UB Irish Lges 1A&B & 2A&B |
| Fri. 22nd to Sun. 24th | Aviva English Premiership (8) |
| | RaboDirect PRO12 (8) |
| | Greene King IPA Championship |
| Sat. 23rd | FRANCE v SA |
| | SCOTLAND v AUSTRALIA |

| | |
|---|---|
| | ITALY v ARGENTINA |
| | English National Leagues |
| | RBS Scottish Premiership |
| | Welsh Principality Premiership |
| | Swalec Welsh Nat Ch/ship |
| Sun. 24th | IRELAND v NZ |
| Fri. 29th | Welsh Principality Premiership |
| Fri. 29th to Sun. 1st Dec. | Aviva English Premiership (9) |
| | RaboDirect PRO12 (9) |
| | Greene King IPA Championship |
| Sat. 30th | WALES v AUSTRALIA |
| | Barbarians v Fiji (Twickenham) |
| | English National Leagues |
| | RBS Scottish Premiership |
| | RBS Scottish National Leagues |
| | RBS Scottish Ch/ship A & B |
| | UB Irish Lges 1A&B & 2A&B |

**DECEMBER 2013**

| | |
|---|---|
| Tue. 3rd | Welsh Principality Premiership |
| Thu. 5th to Sun. 8th | Heineken Cup (3) |
| | Amlin Challenge Cup (3) |
| Sat. 7th | English National Leagues |
| | Swalec Welsh Nat Ch/ship |
| | Swalec Welsh Nat Leagues |
| | UB Irish Leagues 2A&B |
| Sat. 7th and Sun. 8th | British & Irish Cup (3) |
| Thu. 12th | OU v CU (Twickenham) |
| Thu. 12th to Sun. 15th | Heineken Cup (4) |
| | Amlin Challenge Cup (4) |
| Sat. 14th | Swalec Welsh Nat Ch/ship |
| | Swalec Welsh Plate (2) |
| | Swalec Welsh Bowl (3) |
| Sat. 14th and Sun. 15th | British & Irish Cup (4) |
| Fri. 20th and Sat. 21st | Aviva English Premiership (10) |
| | RaboDirect PRO12 (10) |
| Sat. 21st | Greene King IPA Championship |
| | English Nat Leagues 1 & 2 |
| | RFU Cup competitions (3) |
| | RBS Scottish Premiership |
| | RBS Scottish National Leagues |
| | RBS Scottish Ch/ship A & B |
| | Welsh Principality Premiership |
| | Swalec Welsh Nat Ch/ship |
| | Swalec Welsh Nat Leagues |
| Thu. 26th | Greene King IPA Championship |
| | Welsh Principality Premiership |
| Fri. 27th and Sat. 28th | Aviva English Premiership (11) |
| Fri. 27th to Sun. 29th | RaboDirect PRO12 (11) |
| Sat. 28th | Greene King IPA Championship |
| | Swalec Welsh Nat Ch/ship |
| | Swalec Welsh Nat Leagues |

## JANUARY 2014

| | |
|---|---|
| Wed. 1st | Greene King IPA Championship |
| Fri. 3rd to | |
| Sun. 5th | Aviva English Premiership (12) |
| | RaboDirect PRO12 (12) |
| Sat. 4th | English National Leagues |
| | Swalec Welsh Nat Ch/ship |
| | Swalec Welsh Nat Leagues |
| | Swalec Cup (1) |
| | UB Irish Leagues 1A&B & 2A |
| Sat. 4th and | |
| Sun. 5th | Greene King IPA Championship |
| Thu. 9th to | |
| Sun. 12th | Heineken Cup (5) |
| | Amlin Challenge Cup (5) |
| Sat. 11th | English National Leagues |
| | Swalec Welsh Nat Ch/ship |
| | Swalec Welsh Plate (3) |
| | Swalec Welsh Bowl (4) |
| | UB Irish Leagues 2A&B |
| Sat. 11th and | |
| Sun. 12th | British & Irish Cup (5) |
| Thu. 16th to | |
| Sun. 19th | Heineken Cup (6) |
| | Amlin Challenge Cup (6) |
| Sat. 18th | English National Leagues |
| | Swalec Welsh Nat Ch/ship |
| | Swalec Welsh Nat Leagues |
| Sat. 18th and | |
| Sun. 19th | British & Irish Cup (6) |
| Sat. 25th | LV= (Anglo-Welsh) Cup (3) |
| | English National Leagues |
| | RBS Scottish Premiership |
| | RBS Scottish National Leagues |
| | RBS Scottish Ch/ship A & B |
| | Swalec Welsh Nat Ch/ship |
| | Swalec Welsh Nat Leagues |
| | UB Irish Leagues 1A&B & 2B |
| Sat. 25th and | |
| Sun. 26th | Greene King IPA Championship |
| Fri. 31st and | |
| Sat. 1st Feb. | UB Irish Lges 1A&B & 2A&B |
| Fri. 31st to | |
| Sun. 2nd Feb. | Greene King IPA Championship |

## FEBRUARY 2014

| | |
|---|---|
| Sat. 1st | WALES v ITALY (14:30) |
| | FRANCE v ENGLAND (18:00) |
| | RFU Cup competitions (4) |
| | RBS Scottish Premiership |
| | RBS Scottish National Leagues |
| | RBS Scottish Ch/ship A & B |
| Sun. 2nd | IRELAND v SCOTLAND (15:00) |
| Fri. 7th and | |
| Sat. 8th | Aviva English Premiership (13) |
| | Greene King IPA Championship |
| Fri. 7th to | |
| Sun. 9th | RaboDirect PRO12 (13) |
| Sat. 8th | IRELAND v WALES (14:30) |
| | SCOTLAND v ENGLAND (17:00) |
| | English National Leagues |
| | Welsh Principality Premiership |

| | |
|---|---|
| Sun. 9th | FRANCE v ITALY (16:00) |
| Fri. 14th and | |
| Sat. 15th | Aviva English Premiership (14) |
| | UB Irish Lges 1A&B & 2A&B |
| Fri. 14th to | |
| Sun. 16th | Greene King IPA Championship |
| Sat. 15th | English National Leagues |
| | Swalec Welsh Nat Ch/ship |
| | Swalec Welsh Nat Leagues |
| | Swalec Cup (2) |
| Sat. 15th and | |
| Sun. 16th | RaboDirect PRO12 (14) |
| Fri. 21st | WALES v FRANCE (20:00) |
| Fri. 21st to | |
| Sun. 23rd | RaboDirect PRO12 (15) |
| Sat. 22nd | ITALY v SCOTLAND (14:30) |
| | ENGLAND v IRELAND (16:00) |
| | RFU Cup competitions (5) |
| | Welsh Principality Premiership |
| | Swalec Welsh Nat Ch/ship |
| | Swalec Welsh Nat Leagues |
| Sat. 22nd and | |
| Sun. 23rd | Aviva English Premiership (15) |
| Fri. 28th and | |
| Sat. 1st Mar. | UB Irish Lges 1A&B & 2A&B |
| Fri. 28th to | |
| Sun. 2nd Mar. | Aviva English Premiership (16) |
| | RaboDirect PRO12 (16) |
| | Greene King IPA Championship |

## MARCH 2014

| | |
|---|---|
| Sat. 1st | English National Leagues |
| | RBS Scottish Premiership |
| | RBS Scottish National Leagues |
| | RBS Scottish Ch/ship A & B |
| | Welsh Principality Premiership |
| | Swalec Welsh Nat Ch/ship |
| | Swalec Welsh Nat Leagues |
| Fri. 7th to | |
| Sun. 9th | *LV= (Anglo-Welsh) Cup SF |
| Sat. 8th | IRELAND v ITALY (14:30) |
| | SCOTLAND v FRANCE (17:00) |
| | English National Leagues |
| | Welsh Principality Premiership |
| | Swalec Welsh Nat Ch/ship |
| Sat. 8th and | |
| Sun. 9th | Greene King IPA Championship |
| Sun. 9th | ENGLAND v WALES (15:00) |
| Fri. 14th | Welsh Principality Premiership |
| Fri. 14th to | |
| Sun. 16th | *LV= (Anglo-Welsh) Cup Final |
| | UB Irish Lges 1A&B & 2A&B |
| Sat. 15th | ITALY v ENGLAND (13:30) |
| | WALES v SCOTLAND (14:45) |
| | FRANCE v IRELAND (18:00) |
| | English Nat Leagues 1 & 2 |
| | RFU Cup competitions (6) |
| Fri. 21st and | |
| Sat. 22nd | Aviva English Premiership (17) |
| Fri. 21st to | |
| Sun. 23rd | RaboDirect PRO12 (17) |
| | Greene King IPA Championship |

| | |
|---|---|
| Sat. 22nd | English National Leagues |
| | Swalec Welsh Nat Ch/ship |
| | Swalec Welsh Nat Leagues |
| | Swalec Cup QF |
| | Swalec Plate QF |
| | Swalec Bowl QF |
| Sat. 22nd and | |
| Sun. 23rd | UB Irish Lges 1A&B & 2A&B |
| Fri. 28th | BUCS Finals (Twickenham) |
| Fri. 28th and | |
| Sat. 29th | UB Irish Leagues 1A&B |
| Fri. 28th to | |
| Sun. 30th | RaboDirect PRO12 (18) |
| Sat. 29th | English National Leagues |
| | RBS Scottish Cup SF |
| | RBS Scottish Shield SF |
| | RBS Scottish Bowl SF |
| | Welsh Principality Premiership |
| | Swalec Welsh Nat Ch/ship |
| | Swalec Welsh Nat Leagues |
| Sat. 29th and | |
| Sun. 30th | Aviva English Premiership (18) |
| | Greene King IPA Championship |

**APRIL 2014**

| | |
|---|---|
| Thu. 3rd to | |
| Sun. 6th | Heineken Cup QF |
| | Amlin Challenge Cup QF |
| Sat. 5th | English National Leagues |
| | RBS Scottish Pr/ship Play-off |
| | Welsh Principality Premiership |
| | Swalec Welsh Nat Ch/ship |
| | Swalec Welsh Nat Leagues |
| | British & Irish Cup QF |
| Fri. 11th and | |
| Sat. 12th | UB Irish Lges 1A&B & 2A&B |
| Fri. 11th to | |
| Sun. 13th | Aviva English Premiership (19) |
| | RaboDirect PRO12 (19) |
| | Greene King IPA Championship |
| Sat. 12th | English National Leagues |
| | Swalec Welsh Nat Ch/ship |
| | Swalec Welsh Nat Leagues |
| | Swalec Cup SF |
| | Swalec Plate SF |
| | Swalec Bowl SF |
| Fri. 18th and | |
| Sat. 19th | Greene King IPA Championship |
| Fri. 18th to | |
| Sun. 20th | RaboDirect PRO12 (20) |
| Sat. 19th | St George's Day Game (T/ham) |
| | English Nat Leagues 1 & 2 |
| | RFU Cup competitions (7) |
| | RBS Scottish Cup Final |
| | RBS Scottish Shield Final |
| | RBS Scottish Bowl Final |
| | Welsh Principality Premiership |
| | Swalec Welsh Nat Ch/ship |
| | Swalec Welsh Nat Leagues |
| | UB Irish Leagues 1A&B |
| Sat. 19th and | |
| Sun. 20th | Aviva English Premiership (20) |

| | |
|---|---|
| Fri. 25th to | |
| Sun. 27th | Heineken Cup SF |
| | *Amlin Challenge Cup SF |
| Sat. 26th | Greene King IPA Championship |
| | English Nat Leagues 1 & 2 |
| | English Nat Lge 3 Play-off |
| | Welsh Principality Premiership |
| | Swalec Welsh Nat Ch/ship |
| | Swalec Welsh Nat Leagues |

**MAY 2014**

| | |
|---|---|
| Fri. 2nd and | |
| Sat. 3rd | Aviva English Premiership (21) |
| Sat. 3rd | Army v Navy (Babcock Trophy) |
| | English Cty Ch/ship Shield (1) |
| | Swalec Cup Final |
| | Swalec Plate Final |
| | Swalec Bowl Final |
| | British & Irish Cup SF |
| Sat. 3rd and | |
| Sun. 4th | HSBC 7s World Series |
| | (Glasgow) |
| Sun. 4th | RaboDirect PRO12 (21) |
| | National U20 Ch/ship Final |
| | RFU Intermediate Cup Final |
| | RFU Senior Vase Final |
| | RFU Junior Vase Final |
| Fri. 9th to | |
| Sun. 11th | Greene King IPA Ch/ship SF (1) |
| Sat. 10th | Aviva English Premiership (22) |
| | English Cty Ch/ship Shield (2) |
| Sat. 10th and | |
| Sun. 11th | *RaboDirect PRO12 SF |
| | HSBC 7s World Series |
| | (London) |
| Fri. 16th to | |
| Sun. 18th | Greene King IPA Ch/ship SF (2) |
| Sat. 17th | English Cty Ch/ship Shield (3) |
| Sat. 17th and | |
| Sun. 18th | *Aviva English Premiership SF |
| Fri. 23rd | British & Irish Cup Final |
| Fri. 23rd to | |
| Sun. 25th | Heineken Cup Final |
| | Amlin Challenge Cup Final |
| Sat. 24th | English Cty Ch/ship Shield (4) |
| Thu. 29th | Greene King IPA Ch/ship Final (1) |
| Sat. 31st | Aviva English Premiership Final |
| | RaboDirect PRO12 Final |

**JUNE 2014**

| | |
|---|---|
| Sun. 1st | England v Barbarians (TBC) |
| | English County Championship |
| | (Bill Beaumont Cup) Final |
| | English Cty Ch/ship Shield Final |
| Wed. 4th | Greene King IPA Ch/ship Final (2) |

**Key**

RC = Rugby Championship, successor
competition to the Tri-Nations
* indicates dates and times to be confirmed